T0131630

Thriving
beyond
Survival

How to *Know* What You Really Want
and Have *Fun* Getting It

Martha Germann

BALBOA.
PRESS
A DIVISION OF HAY HOUSE

Copyright © 2015 Martha Germann.

All rights reserved. No part of this book may be used or reproduced by any means, graphic, electronic, or mechanical, including photocopying, recording, taping or by any information storage retrieval system without the written permission of the author except in the case of brief quotations embodied in critical articles and reviews.

Balboa Press books may be ordered through booksellers or by contacting:

Balboa Press
A Division of Hay House
1663 Liberty Drive
Bloomington, IN 47403
www.balboapress.com
1 (877) 407-4847

Because of the dynamic nature of the Internet, any web addresses or links contained in this book may have changed since publication and may no longer be valid. The views expressed in this work are solely those of the author and do not necessarily reflect the views of the publisher, and the publisher hereby disclaims any responsibility for them.

All of these experiences are mine; however, some of the names have been changed to protect others' privacy.

Any people depicted in stock imagery provided by Thinkstock are models, and such images are being used for illustrative purposes only. Certain stock imagery © Thinkstock.

Print information available on the last page.

ISBN: 978-1-5043-4145-5 (sc)
ISBN: 978-1-5043-4147-9 (hc)
ISBN: 978-1-5043-4146-2 (e)

Library of Congress Control Number: 2015915657

Balboa Press rev. date: 10/28/2015

Contents

To Joseph Germann, who inspired me to *thrive* in life.

Acknowledgments

I would like to thank all who encouraged and supported me in writing this book. A special thank-you to Marilyn Mathis, who contributed her editing expertise but more importantly her enthusiasm and belief in the message that was instrumental in my picking up a pen to begin with. I want to thank Angie Torres for her graphic designs. Much appreciation to all my beta readers who helped to shape the final words: Becky Bigby, Mary Anne Davis, Jim Embry, Virginia Germann, Bill Lockhart, DeAnna Shires, Tia Short, and Helen Young. And a special thank-you to Jessica Labosco for giving the manuscript one last scrub to make it shiny and Elisabeth, the editor at Balboa Press, for smoothing out the last wrinkles. Thank you, Helen Chouinard, for providing your photography talent.

A big thank-you to my family, who fills me with love and appreciation.

Introduction

I just want to quit.

Jean, my director, who is located in another state, just called to tell me the latest: "The department is reorganizing."

Again? I think to myself. This will be the third time in two years, and each time my situation seems to get worse. The last time our VP decided to reorganize, I lost most of my team. I was merely informed of who was being cut and who was moving to different departments—never consulted, even though I was their manager. I went from a team of five to one employee, Laura.

I brace myself.

"Okay, so what does this mean?" I ask, while the really deep-down part of me doesn't want to know.

"Well, I am not sure what your new role will be. But what I do know is that I will be leaving the company and Laura will start reporting to Barbara."

No! I scream in my head. I adore both my director and my employee. These are the two people who kept me sane during the other reorganizations, and now they are being pulled away from me.

So here I am again being told things are changing but having no idea why. I am feeling really pushed around and not valued. It doesn't make sense. I can see no advantage to me, the department, or the corporation in just rearranging people.

I am ready to quit.

Not as a decision but as a reaction. I want to get away, not just from the situation but from the way I am feeling: powerless.

As sad as this scenario is, the sadder part is that it is not a rare one. When people feel they have no voice in the decisions affecting them, that perception of feeling undervalued can mushroom into feeling hopelessly trapped—in their jobs, their relationships, or their lives. Many would love to quit. Most don't; they may stay, but they disengage or get angry and then possibly ill.

In my case back in 2010, the wacky thing was that I was in the Leadership Development Department. I trained leaders and employees on how to set goals, give feedback, and handle difficult conversations, in essence preventing or dealing with situations that create a hostile environment like the one I was experiencing. I also believe it was because of this background that I was able to find a way out of my emotional trap.

My instinct was to get out of the misery, but just acknowledging my pain wasn't getting me the result I wanted. I began to draw on all the information, tools, and techniques that I'd practiced throughout my career in learning and development. My emotions were at full throttle. Thankfully, my mind rallied to help solve the problem; as I had helped others, this time I was determined to make a difference for myself.

In order to rediscover what had worked for me in the past, I called on what I knew of emotional intelligence, appreciative inquiry, and other disciplines, including the spiritual masters I'd studied earlier in my life. I analyzed the different challenges and accomplishments I had experienced to sift through the components of effective solutions and reapply them to the present.

Looking back, I realize I wasn't doing this like a research scientist, methodically taking notes and compiling data. I did it with that unfocused determination that you get when you are figuring out a nagging word problem or getting to the next level in your favorite video game. I was making connections with information that I hadn't made before. There came a point when I actually had a visual of the way out.

The visual came to me in the form of a model. I drew what was pictured in my head on a sheet of paper so that I would remember it, and I began to use it for the situation at work. With the model, I saw that although it takes being in action to reach any goal, it is our beliefs that fuel the specific actions we take. Failure occurs when we are unaware that our beliefs and actions are misaligned with our intended results. The model not only gave me this awareness, but it gave me a road map back to becoming aligned. I would use it to get to a place where success was guaranteed and I could thrive.

I noticed I was altering how I approached things at work and ultimately how I felt. Though things were still churning in the office, my overall experience was steadily improving. I showed the model to my family and friends to see whether they were able to benefit. They were.

I began presenting to groups and soon heard stories of how using the model allowed my friends and colleagues to get better results and move toward goals and dreams they had all but given up on. My sister started a new business; a friend finally got the promotion that had eluded her for years. People were able to turbo-charge their growth and progress toward goals that were important to them. But more impressively, they were consistently happier while getting there. They were thriving beyond survival.

> "A lot of people think or believe or know they feel (experience)—but that's thinking or believing or knowing; not feeling (experiencing). Almost anybody can learn to think or believe or know, but not a single human being can be taught to feel (experience). Why? Because whenever you think or you believe or you know, you're a lot of other people: but the moment you feel (experience), you're nobody-but-yourself.
>
> To be nobody-but-yourself—in a world which is doing its best, night and day, to make you everybody

else—means to fight the hardest battle which any
human being can fight; and never stop fighting."
—R. Buckminster Fuller

The information in this book is what I have discovered through
applying the model to my own experience. I use the concepts of the
Thriving beyond Survival model every day. I have shared the model
with others who have found it just as useful in their own experiences.
I believe that it can make a difference for you also, but don't just
take my word for it; try out the ideas and see whether they work for
you. Experiment.

In the first part of the book, we will walk through the Thriving
beyond Survival model so that you will be able to see where you are
at any moment, if you are thriving or surviving.

The second half of the book will be all about strategies you can
use to get back to thriving and spend more of your time there.

Throughout the book, I will suggest things you can do to
experience the concepts for yourself. These suggestions will be
designated with this symbol: ☞

What works for me may not work for you, but you won't know
until you give it a try in your own experience, not just in your own
reasoning. Like Fuller said in the above quote, this is about you
being "nobody-but-yourself." This book is not telling you how to
live your life; it is about giving you a different mind-set and some
concepts to make new choices that you may not have known you
had. In this way, you can truly be empowered in creating how you
want your life to be and contribute to the world and others what you
are most suited and excited to contribute. You are the only expert on
your life. This life is yours to experience, and I believe that we each
have the ability to steer that life in the best direction possible. We
cannot control all external circumstances, but we have the power to
strongly influence how situations can turn out for us. For me, that
is thriving. How about you?

PART 1

The Thriving beyond Survival Model

CHAPTER 1

We Are Designed to Thrive

What does it mean to *thrive*?

Think of that time when you were so intrigued and interested in what you were doing that you got lost in the moment. It may have been while you were creating a document, playing an instrument, or having a stimulating conversation. You may have gained a new insight, felt the satisfaction of the progress you were making, or reveled in the ability to do something you'd never been able to do before. You were enjoying not only the experience but also everyone involved. You felt good. You were thriving.

What if you were able to increase the time you spent having these kinds of experiences—that is, *thriving*?

You may have often heard phrases such as, "It is not the situation but how you react to the situation that matters," or, "The only things you truly have control over are your thoughts and emotions." Both of these statements are true, and you may agree with them on an intellectual level, but you may also believe that your situations continually provide exceptions to these tenets. When you feel fear or perceive danger, it may seem that you have no choice—that the reactions and emotions "are just there," and the situation is either staying the same or getting worse. What you need is a different way to see what your options are in a situation. By making only a slight adjustment, you can tune your situation to thriving.

Most people today are stressed. Being stressed out has become the default way of living life. Our reactive emotions are a step up

3

from the numbness we use to protect ourselves from the struggles of life: the demands, the responsibilities, and the need to make increasing amounts of money. Our view of the world is based on a model of drama. The dramatic curve is the formula of most stories, and so we use it to create the stories of our lives.

It's true that drama increases emotions. There is something compelling about a story with a hero struggling against a seemingly insurmountable foe and then being victorious (and in the sequel, there is sure to be a more evil villain and a bigger struggle to keep our interest). If you choose to be in a dramatic story, there is nothing wrong with that. Drama can be exciting. However, it is also a mode where we are neither our most productive nor our most creative, and many people don't know they have another choice. Drama is everywhere—in every news report and in many TV shows, movies, and books. The drama is even hyped and exaggerated in sporting events.

Life, however, does not have to be this way. What if drama was just one of your choices? What if there was another model that you could choose?

Thriving

If you are tired of the perpetual drama and the continual need to fight against someone or something or to look over your shoulder for the next thing that will trip you up, if you are tired of being tired, then you are ready for Thriving beyond Survival.

The Thriving beyond Survival model does far more than simply confirm that how you react to the situation makes all the difference. Whether you are feeling trapped or in the flow, it will reveal the choices you have and give you practical ways to keep choosing to thrive—not just survive.

Choosing to thrive is not a one-time decision. Thriving is a moment-to-moment, conscious choice that gets easier the more you practice. It allows you to grow to the next level and to keep deliberately growing in a direction that is meaningful to you—not in a direction you've been told you have to go, need to go, or should go but in the direction in which you really want to go.

By using this model, you will learn to distinguish two choices you have in each situation: to thrive or to just survive. You may not currently be aware of these choices, in which case you may be reacting in the only way you believe you can.

According to Webster, to *thrive* is to "grow or develop successfully: to flourish or succeed (Merriam-Webster)." This is the choice you can move toward. It's the choice you would want to give to someone you care about—including yourself.

Most of the time, we choose our reaction out of habit and impulse, not from conscious choice. This means our automatic response is set to survival mode. Like the repetition of any skill, as we continue to choose to keep thriving, the choices will become easier and easier. We will experience better and better results, which will allow us to grow in ways we may never have imagined.

Thriving isn't ignoring or denying what is happening around you. Rather, it is truly how you prefer to be and to act, no matter the circumstances. A few months ago, I had the privilege of meeting someone who demonstrates the power of making this choice.

In 2012, Scarlett Lewis had to deal with the fact that her son Jessie was gunned down in the Sandy Hook Elementary School massacre. This is a situation no mother wants to experience. She could hang on to anger, fear, and hatred—and most people would agree that that would be a valid response to this tragic situation—or she could make a different choice.

In her 2014 TEDx talk, Lewis stated that she realized it was an angry thought in the shooter's head at some point that caused the tragedy, and a thought can be changed. Taking a cue from her son's last communications (three scribbled words on a kitchen chalkboard a week before: "nurturing, healing, love") and the words written in snow on her car on his way to school that day ("I love you"), she chose love, even though it would have been easier to stay angry. Every day, she chooses to practice appreciation and forgiveness. She has found her way forward to thriving. She is now the founder of the Choose Love Foundation, which collaborates with professional educators developing school-based educational programs to change our current culture of violence to one of safety, peace, and love for everyone in our world. She is creating a new model to make an old model obsolete.

Scarlett demonstrates that no matter what the circumstances, we always have a choice. We can choose to thrive instead of just survive.

The Thriving beyond Survival Model

In the first part of this book, we will walk through the Thriving beyond Survival model to give you a map of how we experience life, both when thriving and when surviving (figure 1). Once you have a feel for the "territory," you will be able to determine where you are at any moment.

Figure 1: Thriving beyond Survival model

The second part of the book will give you strategies focused on how to get to thriving and how to spend more of your time there.

Get Started—Write a Better Story for Yourself

As the name implies, there are two sides of the Thriving beyond Survival model—the thriving side and the surviving side. But before we describe those two sides, we need to look at some basics of how we operate as human beings—our engine, in a way.

The model starts with our goals.

Vision/Goals/Dreams

If you were able to recreate your life exactly as you wanted it, what would it be like? What would be happening? How would you be feeling? Who would be there?

To do anything, including thriving and growing optimally, you need to move in a direction that you *want* to go. This starts with imagining what you want to do, to experience, and to have. Nothing new was ever created without someone first picturing it in his or her imagination.

We live in a society that values analysis and logic. As a result, people have let their ability to dream and imagine go dormant. At some point, we were told to get our heads out of the clouds and quit daydreaming—to face reality and be logical. School systems and work environments tend to offer higher rewards for the logical mind than the creative mind.

So we have stopped dreaming, and we tend to move toward what is predictable instead of what is preferred. We may still imagine a future for ourselves, but we expect it to be similar to now and closely related to yesterday. We may not realize how much this sidelining of imagination affects the outcome of our present reality, but partly as a result of this, we are stressed, disengaged, and worn out.

Both analysis and logic are useful, but they are not the only skills our minds have that bring us value. We need to get back to using our imaginations and begin to dream again. The imagination can be described as a powerful visualization muscle. If not used, it can atrophy just like physical muscles. This may intimidate some of us because we are either out of practice or afraid of the act of dreaming. As a result, the scope of our dreams narrows and shrivels. We imagine the disappointment of a failed dream or that the contrast between the dream and the reality would be too great. But to thrive, we must start to dream about what we really want and not prepare for a replay or even just a more dramatic version of the present.

Not to worry—you will have a choice. You can stay with what feels certain, safe, and predictable, or you can gradually practice creating a dream and a vision of what you want and then go on to practice the habits that will keep you thriving. You get to decide if the effort is worth it to you.

You can start small. Think of an area in your life that is important to you. What do you want to have, feel, or do in that area that is truly exciting and meaningful for you? Maybe you would like to successfully complete a project and get not only the results you intend but also an outcome where everyone involved is happy and satisfied.

Or you may want to increase your sales in your business next quarter and expand your client base.

Your goal may be built around your relationship with your son or daughter, partner or parent. Maybe you would like to build some understanding and harmony in that personal relationship.

The important thing, in the beginning, is to have a goal that is truly what you want.

Take a deep breath. Use this moment to create a goal for an area in your life.

Now, don't write it down just yet. First, visualize it or verbalize it in your mind.

You have your goal? Great.

The Part that Actions Play

To reach any goal, it is going to take action.

There is something that you will ultimately need to do to reach any goal you came up with.

Vision/Goals/Dreams

Action

Figure 2

In our culture, once a goal is set and written down, we immediately want to focus on the actions. Traditionally, we do this by creating an action plan, setting up a to-do list, and marking things off. This may even be second nature to you, and you may not have considered another method. But today, we are going to look at things a little differently. Why? Because once we identify an action, our focus tends to shift from our goal to the action. Soon, we have so many lists and so much to get done that we forget to see if we have made any progress toward the intended results. Our days are measured by the number of items crossed off our lists. If we have more crossed off than left undone, it was a good day. If there were more things left on the list, it was a bad day, and in neither case have we noticed whether or not we are even going in the right direction.

It Is Not about Always Doing More

Action is important; it is what helps us achieve any goal. The specific goal actually lets us determine the best actions to take next. So it is okay if you think of things that you can start doing to reach your goal, but if your goal is to get a result that you have never gotten before, use that list of things as a guide, not a set of instructions that, if followed faithfully, will guarantee success. If our focus shifts from our goal to just getting things on our list done, then we will find things to put on the list just to cross off. Do the items on that list really move us to our ultimate goal? Focusing on just the actions can divert our attention from our intended outcomes. So we can be doing, doing, doing and not really getting anywhere; in fact, we may actually be getting off course. If you have lost focus on if what you do really matters, you are in an illusion of productivity.

Though this may sound counter to how most people approach or have been taught to do goal setting, the process of creating the action plan and getting to work will not ensure the goal will be reached. What will ensure our success is our ability to stay focused on our goal and the results that we desire. So having a plan is a good start, but do not fall into this illusion of productivity. If you think that now that you have a plan, all you need to do is complete the action items and you will be successful, you may still be stuck, wondering why you are not getting any closer to your ultimate goal. After all, you are getting so many things done!

There was a student I knew who was determined to get A averages in all his classes. He had a goal and was committed to it, but the grades in each of his classes kept going up and down. He spent many hours studying for his tests, which he would pass, but his overall grades still suffered. He even signed up for tutoring to help him get his average up. With all this work and effort, he never realized that he would neglect his homework in one class while he spent all his time and energy studying for a test in another class, which not only gave him a zero in the homework, but he would then have to work harder the next week to study for a test in that other class. He was dedicated and busy but had not stopped to confirm the actions he took were aligned with his goal and helping him progress. He just kept trying to succeed by doing more and more.

Consider that if we create a goal that will give us that new result we are seeking, the one that has eluded us before, we may not know all the actions we need to reach our goal when we create that action plan. If we already knew how to do it, we would have already done it. And following a plan that worked for someone else may not work the same for us. This is a key moment in changing your goal-setting behavior. This will move you in a new direction, so that you do not end up setting a predictable goal based only on the past.

The idea is to take some time to focus on our goal and become aware of how even the existence of that goal changes our attitude, direction, and momentum. When we become consistently mindful of our goal, we can accurately comprehend if we are progressing toward or away from the results we want. If we take action that moves us away from our target, we need to choose different actions, despite what is on our to-do list. And if our focus is on our intended goal, we can choose different actions in the moment. Actions are most effective when they are adjustable and fluid, while we are consciously aware of the feedback that lets us learn and decide on the next action.

So now, go ahead and write your goal down to keep it in mind, without worrying just yet about *how* to accomplish it.

Believing It Can Be Done

> "The most important thing we can
> do is to choose what to believe."
> —Charles Williams

You have a written goal, and you may have some ideas of actions that can get you started. Many people get to this point, maybe even take a step or two and then … stop, never reaching their goals, sometimes giving up on their dreams or visions altogether after only a meager attempt.

Your goals help you determine your plan of action—that is, what to do next to reach your intended results. However, what actually moves you to action and keeps you progressing toward success will not be your goal but what you believe about the goal, the situation, and yourself.

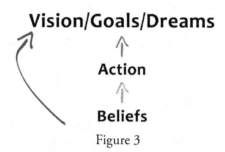

Figure 3

When you believe that you can accomplish something and that you either have the skills or will learn them, and when you believe strongly that you will do it, your beliefs are aligned with the goal, and you get into action with little hesitation. The actions are almost a no-brainer.

However, you may know people who have set a goal or talked about a dream they have. They know some actions they need to take to accomplish their goals but never take a step or stop just after getting started. And no matter how many times you encourage them and tell them they can do it, they still put it off. Give excuses. Sigh and say, "Someday."

This is because their beliefs about the goal or about themselves are still not lined up with what they truly want.

Henry Ford said, "Whether you think you can, or think you can't, you're right."

You may also know people who reached goals that at first seemed impossible.

I remember seeing musician Brandi Carlile and her band perform live for the first time. I've been to many live performances by big-time artists before but had never left a concert feeling so inspired and uplifted. I found myself going to as many of her concerts as I could and found that they consistently had that same quality. I was not the only one feeling that there was some magic in her performance; many reviewers commented on the same quality that I experienced.

I began to wonder, what was it about this artist that captured my attention? What was it about her music that gave me such a lift? What was her mojo? It wasn't about the lyrics of her songs; many of her songs are on the rather sad side.

Then it dawned on me that when Brandi and her band are performing, she is totally aligned in her journey of making music and her belief that it is what she is here to do. She is thriving, and she reminds those of us in the audience that thriving is what we are designed for.

In looking at her story, you can find evidence that she is out to thrive. She is not a big mainstream performer playing big stadiums, but there is still that fairytale quality. When forming her band, she declared to her new band mates that they would have a record contract within a year, and they were later signed with Sony. She has performed with her childhood music heroes like Elton John and Dave Matthews, has been backed up by symphonies, and has had her songs featured on the hit TV show *Grey's Anatomy*. She formed her own charity foundation that aligns with her commitment to give back to communities. She stays true to who she is and what it is that she loves to do.

Her focus was not about earning a living with her music, it was full on about making music and living.

When your beliefs are aligned with your goal, your conscious and unconscious brain looks for options and solutions for obtaining your desired results. You begin to use your imagination and creativity to find ways to achieve your goal and enjoy seeing the progress toward success.

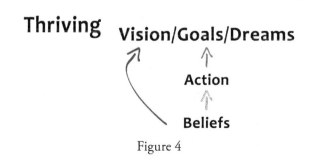

Figure 4

Here's what it looks like when your beliefs are aligned with your goal:

- You believe that the goal is meaningful and its accomplishment is beneficial for you.
- You believe it is worth your time and effort.
- You believe that attaining the goal is possible (even if you don't know exactly how to achieve it yet).
- You believe you have or can acquire the ability to achieve the goal.

Suddenly, taking the necessary action becomes a fulfilling task, perhaps even an enjoyable one. You just do what needs to be done, and the effort itself becomes exciting as you progress toward the goal.

Having your beliefs aligned with your goal and taking actions toward that goal make up the formula for thriving.

It seems simple, but beliefs, the key to thriving, are also tricky because our beliefs can also get us into a feeling of just surviving.

Beliefs as Habits

A belief is a thought that you habitually think to the point that you consider it true.

If you hold something as true, it is in a way locked in according to your brain. Your worldview will reflect that "truth." This works to your benefit when your belief is aligned with what you want. When your truth is that you can do anything you put your mind to or that you are a quick learner and things are always going your way, you are swift to get into action and take steps toward your goal. Our consciously chosen beliefs that shape our values, our faith, and what is important to us have tremendous power in guiding our behavior.

But not all the beliefs that we carry around with us are beneficial because not all of them have been consciously chosen.

You have been creating beliefs about yourself, about your life, and about the world around you since you were born. Some of those beliefs—those habits of thought—have become like many of your physical habits, unconscious. For instance, because I know that brushing my teeth twice a day is beneficial, I have created a habit of the activity. Remembering to do the task is automatic and takes no effort.

The value of creating a habit is that you no longer have to use valuable brain energy putting something into action. It has changed to an unconscious effort where the action becomes automatic. Now we are able to free up our consciousness for more important processing. I don't have to think about the action of brushing my teeth; I just do it.

There may be physical habits that we have created without consciously being aware of them until someone points them out. And some of these are not beneficial. I once taught a presentation course where one of the participants had a habit of making mouth noises in place of other people's habit of saying "um." This gentleman would do clicking, sucking, and other noises that were distracting to his audience, all of which he was totally unaware. At first, he didn't believe the feedback. It wasn't until he saw and heard himself on video that he was able to catch himself and change the habit.

Some physical habits are created deliberately, and others are not. Thought habits are the same; some of these habits you purposefully create, and others are picked up unconsciously. And those thoughts that have become a habit form your beliefs.

Beliefs shape the way you view your world and how you respond to events. Some of those beliefs are beneficial and help you to stay on track—such as a belief that "it is always good to review your work" or "I can do this."

And then there are some unconscious beliefs that are not aligned with your goals, such as a belief that "things never really work out for me" or "I have no real power here." These beliefs are not ones that you would consciously create or choose, but you may have picked them up unconsciously and carry them with you anyway.

Beliefs will drive your actions. So when a belief gets triggered and fits the current situation you are in but is not in alignment with your goal, your actions will be inconsistent with your intended results. And because these are usually unconscious habits, you may not even realize that your actions are getting you off track, veering you away from your goal. You honestly believe that you are doing everything you are able to and the best that you can.

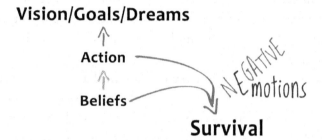

Figure 5

This is why many of you may be spending more time in survival mode instead of thriving. If you are not aware you are out of alignment, it becomes very difficult to get back on track, and you feel stuck or resigned.

The good news is that you do have a wonderful indicator that lets you know when you are aligned with your goals or not. That indicator is your emotions. When you are on track and your beliefs and actions are aligned with your vision and goals, you feel good. And whenever you are veering off course, you have a built-in alarm that alerts you every time if you are paying attention. This ingenious alarm is your negative emotions.

But in order to understand what happens when we get off track and the alarm goes off, we need to first understand where our beliefs come from and how they drive our actions, often without our realizing it. The next chapter will describe how we create and acquire our beliefs.

CHAPTER 2

Where Do We Get Our Beliefs?

Humans are all unique. Each one of us has different experiences and a unique point of view. I may have been at the same place at the same time and experienced the same event as you, but how we view and understand that event will not be the same. The experiences may be similar, so we can relate to it with each other, but it will never be identical. This is because of our unique perspective and our cocktail of inner beliefs that we have acquired from birth up to this point in time.

Let me give you a picture of what is going on.

As you are going about your life, you are constantly taking in data. You are essentially one big sensory organ that is picking up information from the world around you. According to researcher Timothy D. Wilson, author of *Strangers to Ourselves*, you have eleven million data points coming into your brain at any moment (and this may be a very conservative number) (Wilson, 2009). Everything you taste and smell and hear and think, even your emotions while doing so, are being picked up and processed in your brain. With all the sensory receptors you have, you are able to take in a massive amount of information. However, your conscious brain cannot possibly deal with and process eleven million pieces of data. You would be overwhelmed.

Thankfully, your unconscious brain is doing most of the processing of those eleven million data points and deciding and filtering which is the most important for your conscious brain to be aware of in order for you to be effective at this moment (figure 6). Your filtering system is excellent at this; even the most advanced supercomputer does not come close to what your brain can do. According to Kwabena Boahen, PhD, a Stanford University professor and director of the Brains in Silicon Research Laboratory, the brain is able to do more calculations per second than even the fastest computer (Thompson, 2013). He explains that though the brain makes a single calculation much slower than a supercomputer, it can actually execute more calculations per second because the networks of neurons actually work together to simultaneously solve many problems at once. This means that the brain is making connections and finding solutions creatively that a computer has no way of doing. This human capability allows for creativity and conceptualization of complex, real-world ideas.

As you go about your day, your brain is constantly scanning, processing, and determining what information gets through to your conscious awareness. And the maximum amount of data that the unconscious brain filters to the conscious brain, according to Wilson, is forty. Forty is the maximum number of data points available to your consciousness when you are thinking clearest and are most open to your surroundings. This means that even in the best of circumstances, there is a lot of information that you have no conscious awareness of. A lot.

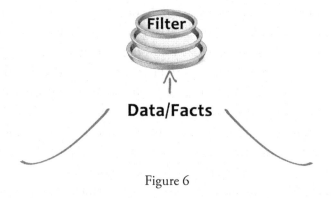

Figure 6

What gets filtered to your conscious mind is what you have stored or programmed as your goals, beliefs, and dangers.

A Working Filter

This filter system is a good thing. You rely on it to stay focused and functional, and to not go totally insane by trying to deal with eleven million pieces of information. Most of us can't even remember a grocery list with seven items.

To give you an example of how well you filter, let's pretend that I have taken you to an overpass of a busy highway and given you an assignment—to count all the blue cars that went under the bridge for an hour starting at seven in the morning. After a few minutes, you would get your process down and be very efficient at counting all those blue cars. You'd probably be confident after the hour that you had an accurate number.

But what if, at the end of the hour, I ask you to tell me how many red cars you saw instead?

You wouldn't have a clue. You would not have seen the red cars. Those red cars would have been filtered right out because they were not part of your goal. Your brain in its wisdom disregarded the information to keep your attention on the blue cars.

Your goals are an important factor that your unconscious filter uses when determining what information it will send to your conscious awareness. Your filter will also sift through any beliefs that may seem related to the goal and situation as well as any dangers you need to be alerted to.

When you were given the task of counting the blue cars, the beliefs your unconscious may have considered relevant and triggered might have included the following:

This is a simple task that I can do with no problem.
This is a silly use of my time.
I have been told to do this by an authority, so I need to do it.

If and how well you do the task will be driven by those types of beliefs. These beliefs come from your experience, culture, parents, teachers, and the media. Some of your beliefs may not be beliefs that you would have chosen for yourself, but they were told to you over and over until you unconsciously made them a part of your filtering system.

Interpreting What Gets through Your Filter

When your conscious brain gets the data that your unconscious brain filtered, you don't look at the information objectively and then take action on that raw data. Instead, you take that data and interpret and add meaning to it. You want to connect the dots and have it make sense to your worldview. You incorporate it into your own life story.

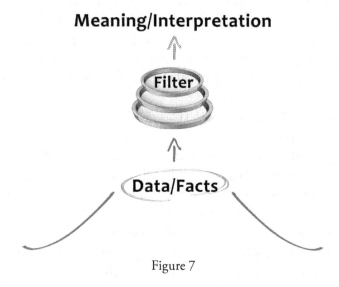

Meaning/Interpretation

Filter

Data/Facts

Figure 7

And you do this automatically, each and every time.

To go back to our example of the blue cars, perhaps you saw a lot more blue cars at the top of the hour and not as many at the bottom of the hour, closer to eight in the morning. You may be thinking, *Maybe this means blue-car drivers get up early and get to work on time; they are the go-getters.*

You want things to make sense and fit in with what you believe is happening, so you fill in any blanks from what you know and have experienced in the past. You connect dots and even make up dots when some are missing in order to make unknowns or spaces connect to fit your story. And sometimes you will alter your story a little to fit the new data. That is how we learn, by making adjustments to what the information means to us. Sometimes the adjustments are small; other times they are transformative. When our story changes, so do we.

A Belief Is Born

From the interpretation of the data that we filter, we create a belief of what is going on and needs to be done (figure 8). So it is from the belief that we take action, not the data. Now you may see what I meant when I said it is not the goal but our beliefs that move us to action. We may believe that those blue-car drivers are the ones to trust, so if we are going to hire someone or look for someone to trust to be on time, an action we might take is to ask them what color car they drive.

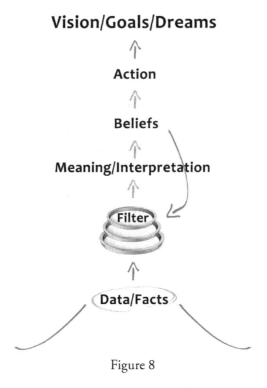

Figure 8

21

This automatic process of filtering data, interpreting, and creating a belief that we then take action on happens in a blink of an eye; it's really ingenious if you think about it. There are times when we want to take action without a whole lot of analysis. Those are times when we want to stay alive.

Around life or death survival, it makes sense. It's about alerting us to a danger, and it is at those times that we want to act quickly.

When a projectile comes hurtling toward your head, you don't spend time wondering if it is soft or not; you just duck. If a tiger runs toward you, you won't spend time wondering if it is friendly or hungry; you take action to save your life. That need to avoid death may have you avoid that dark alley at this time of night. This process allows our brain to quickly get us into action without a lot of thought or conscious analysis.

So this automatic process of jumping from a belief to immediate action has kept humans alive for a very long time.

When you are feeling safe, you are able to see that how you are interpreting the data is creating or contributing to a belief. In the example about the blue cars, you know you are not in danger during this activity. This makes a difference when you begin fitting your beliefs in with the rest of what you know. When you think, *Blue-car drivers are trustworthy*, you probably see it as a belief, not as a truth. You know you can check your theory out, get more facts, do more research, and adjust your belief appropriately.

When there is no fear of danger, you can see the creation of a belief as an interpretation, a hypothesis or theory, and look for more information to get a bigger picture. You are able to adjust your interpretation without much resistance. Learning takes place, you grow your perspective, and you adjust your actions to get to your goal (figure 9).

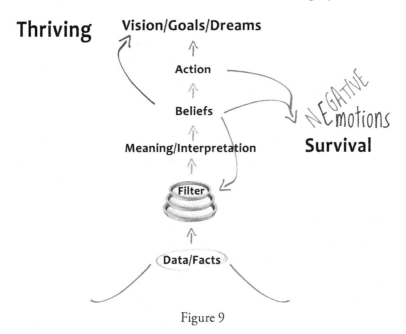

Figure 9

Seeing Danger

When a belief that you are in danger is triggered, you go into an automatic response without much conscious thought. What makes it tricky is that the belief of danger is usually so powerfully attached to the emotion of fear and has been reinforced throughout your life that it no longer occurs as a belief but as a truth. This means that it is more hardwired into your brain, more locked in. And if what is happening is a truth, your options become very limited.

I remember coming out of a meeting, and as I watched my employee, Mark, come toward me, I could tell he was upset. Mark was an even-tempered, gentle man, and I had never seen him get outwardly mad, but in this moment he was red in the face, and I could just imagine steam coming out of his ears like it does in cartoons.

"What's going on?" I asked.

"They changed the locks on the door to the library, and I can't get in." Mark spat out, "The manager is not answering my calls, and no one will give me any explanation. They are trying to take the room away from us. They can't do this—we did not give them ownership of the room. We just said they could use it, and now I need to get in there, and I can't!"

Mark had not only called the other manager repeatedly but also harassed some of her employees, looking for an explanation about why the locks were changed on a room that our department owned and that contained our resources. We had recently agreed to let this other department use some of the available space for a big project they were working on. Mark was now sure that they were executing a hostile takeover of the valuable space. He had even drafted a letter to the division's VP to complain. He was taking actions from his fear and belief about what was happening as if it were the truth.

After I was able to calm him down and get him focused on something else, I tracked down the other manager and found that there was a perfectly good explanation. It turned out that the project they needed the room for involved converting personnel files from paper to digital. She had not been expecting the files until the next week but got word right before going into a meeting that they were going to be delivered the next day, and the room was not secure yet for those types of confidential files. She put in an order to have the locks changed so that she was sure that no one else, not even housekeeping, had keys except for us. She thought she would have time to let us know before the request of the lock change was fulfilled, but maintenance did it in record time. She handed me our keys.

Mark was in survival mode and felt a danger. He had an emotion that sent him into attack mode as if his life depended on it. And when you step back to think about it, most of us in our culture do not face life-threatening situations during our usual day-to-day activities. We will, however, have the same physical, emotional, and mental responses to the things that we believe are dangers, as if they mean life or death, just as Mark did. This puts us into a frame of mind that has us in what I have been calling survival mode. When we are in survival mode and react to a perceived danger that is not immediately life or death, we fall into the game of drama.

Now that we have an idea of how our beliefs play a major part in driving our actions and behaviors, in the next two chapters we will see how to recognize how we tend to behave when we are surviving and when we are thriving so that we can begin to have a choice in how we want to act in every situation.

CHAPTER 3

The Game of Drama—When We Are Just Surviving

O ur beliefs create the filters that cause us to perceive what is happening in a certain way. Some of the major beliefs we filter for are those that we have determined are dangers. When we feel danger, we have an automatic fear response that puts us into fight or flight.

Imagine you are driving to work in the usual morning traffic. You look down for a second to change the station on the radio, and when you look up, you see the two bright red brake lights of the car in front of you, much too close. You hit your own brakes and swerve to the right, narrowly missing the other driver's back fender. While you sit there breathing quickly, feeling the tingling of the adrenaline coursing through your veins, you know that you have just experienced your automatic response to danger, that same fight-or-flight experience as being chased by the metaphorical tiger. After realizing you are safe, you take a deep breath and shake it off. Thankfully, for most of us, these types of true life-or-death moments are rare and not an everyday occurrence.

On the other hand, there are those times when we get that phone call from our boss telling us that the due date on the project that we were struggling with has been moved up. Our body will react to the news in the same way it did in the traffic situation. The adrenaline will be released, our blood flow will be directed to our muscles and away from our internal organs, we will tense up to be ready to pounce or flee, and when we hang up the phone, not realizing we are in fight or flight, we don't just shake off the response, even though we are not in any physical danger. This is us in what I call everyday survival mode.

When we believe we are in any type of danger, whether it is a danger of getting crushed by a falling rock, or a danger of failing in a pursuit we are invested in, or not being shown the respect we believe we deserve, our bodies react the same way. And because we have instances like the call from our boss happening throughout our day, we now feel like being in everyday survival is normal. It is just the way life is, and we tend to be in an automatic state of fight or flight so often that we don't even notice it.

Most times our reactions while in everyday survival are not appropriate or in the best interest of reaching our goals, and we don't feel like we have any choice because, in the moment, it really feels like life or death.

When we go into survival mode, our actions and behaviors will match whatever belief is triggered, no matter what our primary goals may be.

We play out the game of drama.

Let me tell you a story.

Let's meet Mabel. As a business analyst in her corporation, she has spent the last five years building her reputation as a valuable employee. She is the highest producer on her team and is the one everyone comes to when they need to resolve a tough issue.

Today Mabel is getting a new manager.

Mabel gets to work early and gets busy on the project at hand; she wants to make a good impression.

As she is typing up the report that is due at the end of the day, Mabel feels a sharp, stinging pull on her right ring finger and realizes that she just broke a fingernail so close to the cuticle that it starts to bleed. Typing is not only messy, it's a bit painful. To be able to fully focus on her report, Mabel knows she will need to take care of this distraction. She reaches into her desk drawer and grabs her modest brown purse, searches for a minute, and pulls out her manicure set. She cuts the damaged nail with the scissors and pulls out the emery board to smooth the edges to prevent snagging her clothing. Right as she begins filing down her nail, up walks the new manager.

What do you think the new manager's reaction might be to the scene and to Mabel? Most people are sure that the manager will believe that Mabel is a slacker, not getting her work done. We have a cultural stereotype of ladies at their desks filing their nails, and this supervisor may have had his share of loafers.

His first reaction may be to say sarcastically, "I see you are working hard," and give an "I've got my eyes on you" look.

The manager may now have a belief that Mabel is a slacker, and if this produces a strong reaction in him, his filter for Mabel will be to look for all the times that she is not producing.

Mabel feels embarrassed and upset because she believes that she has made a bad impression. She is now worried and afraid that her reputation as a top performer is being threatened.

Both Mabel and her boss are in everyday survival mode and may not even notice.

When we sense dangers or threats, our higher brain functioning shuts down. The limbic system takes over, and the only choice it will give us in this moment to save our lives is fight or flight.

Survival
Negative Emotions
Fear/Danger
Fight/Flight

However, in a situation like Mabel's and many that you face in your day-to-day work environment, neither fight nor flight is the best choice. But the response is automatic. And your whole physiology will match the fight-or-flight response.

Humans produce adrenaline and cortisol when we sense danger. Our heart rates speed up, our breathing becomes shallow, we get tunnel vision, losing some peripheral sight, and our muscles tense up. We are stressed and ready to pounce or flee. How it looks in the office or even in line at the grocery store is that we either yell and attack with a sarcastic comment like Mabel's supervisor, or we throw up our hands with a sense of helplessness and withdraw or disengage like Mabel. The emotions that we feel are negative emotions, such as anger, frustration, being overwhelmed, guilt, hurt, and the list goes on. These emotions have fear or a need to protect ourselves as the basis.

There is nothing wrong with the emotions you feel when you sense danger. Emotions are not only a vital part of the human experience, they are signals from your brain that something is either going well when you feel positive, or not how you want it to be when you feel negative. Negative emotions are a signal for you to pay attention. If you didn't have negative emotions, you couldn't progress. You would never know when to adjust.

Your brain automatically wants to protect you from perceived danger that it detects. It knows to sound the alarm because you have programmed your filter to be on the lookout for certain things that you determined are a danger. Many of these signals were established when you were young and more vulnerable or by things that you were told over and over when learning to fit within your current culture. The strongest signals were created when you were in a situation that caused you pain, whether emotional or physical, and so you set up a filter to alert you to that type of situation. The alarm that is sounding now is based on how similar this situation is to a past experience. It has narrowly selected the data you now see.

Mabel believes her new manager thinks she is a slacker and all her hard work in building her reputation as a good performer is being threatened.

A couple weeks after that first meeting, as Mabel is working at her desk, her coworker Clara comes by at the end of her break to ask for help on an issue. Mabel is happy to help because this is when she feels most valuable. The two colleagues work together until the problem is resolved. When Clara gets up to go back to her desk, she forgets about the magazine she had with her on her break and unintentionally leaves it lying on Mabel's desk. Mabel doesn't notice the magazine until she sees her new manager coming up the aisle and watches him look at the magazine and then look up at her as he walks by.

Mabel sits mortified. She is sure she knows what that look on his face means, and she feels a sense of hopelessness start to simmer. She just can't catch a break with this guy.

What do you, as a human, do when your body is signaling that something is a physical danger, even though it is not? Your spouse criticizes your cooking. Your boss hands you a new project that you have no idea how to accomplish. Your coworker gets the promotion instead of you.

You do the same thing you would do if you saw a rabid dog coming at you. You go into fight or flight. Your brain literally shuts down its higher thought processes and gives you those two choices. And—no surprise—any time you spend in survival mode, those are your only two choices, to attack or withdraw.

If, after you went into the initial fight-or-flight reaction and the original threat was gone, you let the blood flow back into your brain and you began to think more broadly and calmly, your behavior would be more aligned with your overall goals, more appropriate to the situation. But in these everyday survival situations, you can't shake it off like you do in those obvious life-or-death situations like narrowly missing a head-on collision or stumbling down the stairs. Being a human being and possessing memory and imagination, you don't just see the situation at hand, because your emotions immediately throw the past and future at you. You remember all the similar situations that happened before in your life and how badly they turned out, and you picture the future and what you are afraid will happen next and/or what it will mean about you. You keep the situation dangerous in your head and keep feeling threatened. And these types of situations keep piling up throughout the day, compounding each other and your sense of being in danger.

What We Do When in Everyday Survival Mode

Being social, your impulse when in survival mode is usually to pick up the phone and call a friend or coworker to tell them what just happened. Other people need to be aware of the danger and help you survive.

This is what Mabel does; she calls several people and tells them the story—her interpretation—of how the situation with her new manager is going horribly.

Mabel will get one of three responses from this activity.

Mabel starts with her best friend, Joyce, and begins her story, "Things with my new manager are just awful. I can't catch a break with him. He thinks I'm a slacker, and he wouldn't even talk to me."

The frustration is clear in her voice as she goes on to describe the situation in detail.

"You need to lay low and not rock the boat," Joyce responds firmly. "He will have his eye on you, looking for any small mistake. I know those types. You might want to get your resume updated. Soon."

Now Joyce is upset along with Mabel and giving her advice to prepare to leave, which seems to be what Mabel has in mind too.

Joyce's response is one of flight.

Next Mabel calls her husband, Greg, and tells the story again, and as she recounts the situation, her belief about what is happening seems even truer now, and with the reaction from Joyce confirming her worst fears, this retelling is even more dramatic. Mabel is sure that she is being treated totally unfairly.

Greg is feeling the same indignation as Mabel, but he advises a different response from Joyce's.

"You shouldn't be treated like that," he says with a heated voice. "You need to go in and demand the respect that you deserve. He can't be making judgments so soon. You are the best he's got over there. If this keeps up, you need to go to HR."

Greg's response is one of fight.

Mabel is now sure that her career is in jeopardy and makes another call, this time to her sister. Her sister, however, is not as drawn into the situation as Joyce and Greg are and gives a third response, one more solution-oriented.

"Wow, you are really upset about this," her sister states calmly. "Let's take a step back and see what actually happened and come up with ideas to resolve this situation. Let's build your confidence back up."

But this is not the response that Mabel is looking for when she is in survival mode.

"But you don't understand!" Mabel yells. "You don't understand who I am dealing with and what I have had to go through. I thought you had my back. I thought you were on my side."

Mabel is actually feeling unsupported and abandoned by her sister, seeing her response as a new threat.

When you are building your story of what you believe is going on and reliving the danger that has you feeling fight or flight, you are not looking for solutions. You are already clear on the only two courses of action that are available to you. It is not options for a solution that you are gathering; it is agreement that the situation is a danger. You are rallying your allies, forming your army. You are seeing who is with you and who is against you. And if someone does not agree with how dreadful things are, then they fall in the against-you column.

Survival
Negative Emotions
Fear/Danger
Fight/Flight
Agreement
Allies/Enemies

You need allies in order to fight your enemy, to track down and trap the metaphorical tiger, or provide you with protection until you can counterattack. For, of course, if you perceive danger, it is because there is an enemy out there that you need to destroy.

This enemy, your tiger, could be your boss, coworker, the company, time, a project, another department, your spouse, your kids, your mother, the government, yourself—the list is endless. The enemy is whatever you believe is causing you to feel in danger at the moment.

With this search for allies, you are also reinforcing the belief to your brain that this situation and any others like it are a danger. You are creating and reinforcing a habit of thought. A story you tell yourself over and over becomes truer for you. You become more invested in what you believe is happening.

Where We Keep Getting Stuck

Now at this point, you are still experiencing negative emotions. Even though you have gathered some allies who agree with you and you are feeling some justification, you are also still feeling the original negative emotions. You are becoming more certain that you are right. You are right that something is wrong, and it is the enemy's fault. You are not only feeling justified; you are feeling righteous.

You now believe that you are fighting the good fight.

Survival
Negative Emotions
Fear/Danger
Fight/Flight
Agreement
Allies/Enemies
Right/Wrong

You feel like you are fighting for your life through your self-respect and your self-esteem. You feel totally justified and righteous. It feels like the most productive thing that you can be doing. This is what I believe gets us stuck in survival mode.

After all, you are the good guy in your story. Those times you can say, "Aha, see there, see what they just did—I told you I was right," you may know as that feeling of righteousness. It is addictive. It gives you a cause that is hard to give up. I call this my "sick glee."

So you continue the fight-or-flight response, ever more convinced that you are right that this is truly a danger.

Looking for the Proof

You have gathered allies willing to support you in your good fight. You are clear that you are right about what is wrong about this situation and who is to blame. It is at this time that you start your campaign of searching for proof and evidence so that you can show the world (or some authority) how right you are. This search for proof and evidence now becomes your primary goal and activity: prove the enemy is wrong and deserves to be annihilated. You feel you need to track down and trap your version of the tiger at all cost.

Studies by Hart, Lozanov, Nadel, and Leonard show that the brain, when threatened, uses less higher-order thinking skills and resorts to the fastest and most survival-oriented part of the brain, the reptilian brain stem. Researchers O'Keefe and Nadel also revealed that with any perceived threat, the brain does the following (Jhensen, 1995):

- loses its ability to take in subtle clues from the environment
- reverts to the familiar tried-and-true behaviors
- loses some of its ability to perceive relationships and patterns
- is less able to do the higher-order thinking skills
- loses some memory capacity
- tends to overreact to stimuli in an almost phobic way

So when in survival mode, you gather the facts that support your position; you get your allies marching with you, watching for when more evidence presents itself that proves that your enemy is wrong. It feels like you are being productive. This is work that you feel needs to be done. You are putting a lot of energy and thought into this campaign.

Survival
Negative Emotions
Fear/Danger
Fight/Flight
Agreement
Allies/Enemies
Right/Wrong
Proof and Evidence

You may have experienced those times where you are not able to go to sleep or pay attention to your work or whatever is happening at the moment because the scenario keeps replaying in your head, and you think to yourself, *I should have seen that coming.* And you think back for any evidence that you can use to prove you are right. When I describe this, some of you may not think that you put your time into just proving that you are right, that what you do is truly fighting the good fight. You can certainly see this behavior in your coworker, or mother, or that other person who seems to always be up in arms with a complaint of how things are going wrong, and it is someone else's fault, and in response to any suggestion you give, they insist that it won't work. Remember that when you are in survival mode, it feels real. It feels like you are following the only course of action possible. When you have the thought, *I don't have any other choice*, let it signal you that you are in survival mode.

How This Affects Your Filter

As you become more convinced that things are wrong, you are also programming your filter to find evidence and hone in on any proof that you can find that you are right. And your filter is very good; it will find any fact or detail that you can use as proof that your story is true. It will also filter out any data that is to the contrary. Data that may present a different story or fresh options will not be visible to you, just like the red cars were not visible in our earlier example.

So in Mabel's good fight, her next action is to find all the proof and evidence. When Mabel's manager points out her declining performance, she sees it as proof that he believes that she is slacking and that he is out to ruin her reputation. What she doesn't see is that because she has been distracted by the situation, she made mistakes that she would have caught and easily corrected before. She is not aware of all the time she has spent on the phone complaining to her allies, which has caused her to get behind in her work.

She keeps thinking about her situation, even when away from work. The scenarios keep replaying over and over in her head, and it keeps her up at night. She feels trapped and exhausted.

Mabel is caught up in the drama.

She is still not feeling good. She is no longer having fun in her job, and she sees it all as the manager's fault.

Feeling Trapped in the Drama

When you are in survival mode, it shades everything else. If the situation that has you triggered at work looks dire, things at home start to look a little murky too. Your whole life appears to have a haze around it, and your energy feels depleted. You want to get out of the feeling and the situation, and because it is making you cranky, you dig yourself in even deeper. You are feeling the stress, but you keep getting drawn into your drama.

Drama. Our brains love it and are drawn to it. Storytellers have used the drama cycle to draw us into a story. Advertisers create drama to convince us that we need their products to save us. A key to creating marketing material is to tell us the bad news, what is wrong with us or the world, then bring in the hero (the product or personality) that will save the day.

It is the same in movies and books. We get hooked into the tragedy, the conflict, the bad situation, and we are not satisfied until the hero comes swooping in. We want justice to be served. We feel vindicated when we see the bad guy get told off, sent to jail, or blown to smithereens.

Drama is not a bad thing; it is sometimes useful. I used a dramatic story about Scarlette Lewis to open the book. It becomes limiting, however, when it becomes an all-encompassing thing. Drama is all about the story you are telling, the interpretation you are giving to the situation. And you are usually only seeing it from one side: the perspective of the victim or the hero, whom you identify with.

There is usually a clear demarcation between the good guy and the bad guy in movies and books. When you create your story, your drama, if there is an enemy, you will want to create a clear demarcation that separates you from the enemy. So he/she, they, or it has to be evil, unreasonable, tainted, etc. You don't want to hear their side of the story because you know it has to be the opposite of yours. And if it isn't, you will make sure it becomes the opposite.

If you have ever seen people change their point of view to further separate themselves from their foes, you have seen this in action.

When you are in the drama, fighting the good fight and working to bring your enemy to justice, you are expending a lot of emotion, energy, and time. And you are still as angry, if not more so, as when you were first triggered.

We spend time and energy tracking down that metaphorical tiger to show all the wrong it has done and determine where it will be next so that we can trap it. But we end up being the ones in the trap.

We are taking action, but what is not getting done is any action consistent with our original goal or vision. We completely lose sight of what we really want and what is truly meaningful for us, or we consciously decided to put it on hold because winning this fight seems so much more important.

But is it?

Mabel believes that she now has a boss that doesn't like her, and there is nothing she can do about it. Things just seem to be getting worse.

What Is Really Happening?

Everybody has different unconscious beliefs that may get triggered and send them off track of their goals, all the while believing that they are productively fighting the good fight. The belief may be that there is never enough time, that they are not respected or being valued, or the belief may be based around the need to be perfect or to always win.

Whatever the belief, when we feel that there is a situation that fits this belief, we feel a negative emotion and go into survival mode. We fight or run away. We look for agreement from allies and make plans to gang up on our enemy. We spend time and energy looking for proof and evidence.

But here is the kicker: no matter what the belief seems to be, at the heart of it is *this* belief that we are afraid is true:

"I can't have or don't deserve what I want."

So every time you are triggered and feel you are not being valued or not getting respect, every time you feel threatened and it is not a life-or-death situation, what you are really afraid of is that *this* is a situation in which you believe

"I can't have or don't deserve what I want."

And all this time and energy that you are expending is spent on proving that you are right that you can't have or don't deserve what you want, and it is the enemy's fault (figure 10).

Even if you win this fight, all you win is being right that you can't have what you want.

No wonder you feel trapped and stuck.

Figure 10

And you get no relief, because whether you destroy your tiger or flee and quit, your filter is still set to look for similar situations that will trigger the same reaction and fear. That belief that triggered you in the first place is still there and has just been reinforced. Your life has an underlying worry—that you can never have what you want—and your filter is always on the lookout for evidence to support it. So even if you get rid of the tiger, if you still have the belief, there will *always* be another tiger.

It's Our Perception

I have found in my own experience that when I get triggered and defensive, it has always been around things about myself that I am not confident about. I remember coming to this realization when I got a poison-pen e-mail from a woman whom I considered a friend. I spent time listening to her issues and shared things going on in my own life. She actually was instrumental in getting me the job I had at that time. I trusted her, and here was this letter that was telling me I was intrusive and not liked by mutual friends. It came out of the blue, and I remember the feeling of getting kicked in the gut.

I cried—okay, I bawled.

Here it was. My worst fear. Someone thinks I am not a good person. Here is the proof I was afraid would surface. The evidence that when I think I am being supportive and making a difference, I am really just spouting gobbledy-gook and bullying people.

In this moment, all the memories of the people who loved and valued me vanished. My brain skewed things my friends had said as just patronizing me, holding back the truth so that they wouldn't hurt my feelings by telling me how really inept I truly was. Even they appeared as not truly my friends by keeping the truth from me; I began to suspect everybody in my life as the enemy. I was surrounded by tigers.

I was feeling the full frontal attack of my fear of not being a good friend or advisor to the people most important in my life, the thing that I wanted most.

And through this turmoil as I was delving into my self-loathing, I consciously saw that I was the one doing the loathing. This e-mail wasn't a spark; it was the tinder that got the already-present embers blazing. It was as if I looked up at who was beating me up and instead of seeing the face of my accuser, I saw my own condemning eyes.

It was in that moment that I realized I really didn't care what the author of the e-mail thought about me—or really, what anyone else might think. I am most concerned and worried about how I see myself, and the only reason I pay attention to what others think is to use it as proof of what I *fear* is the truth.

My fear was not that it would prove to other people how minor a person I was; I was just using them to prove it to myself. The war was not really with anyone but myself.

Here is what I was able to distinguish. I know for a fact that I have blue eyes, so I don't need to prove it to anyone, and I am not scanning the horizon to see if there might be someone who may question the color. And if someone were to come up and tell me I had brown eyes, I would feel no need to get defensive. I would just shrug and say, "Whatever." I don't fear that I might not have blue eyes, but when I was triggered, I did fear that I might not make a difference.

A few years after my discovery that whenever I got hurt or defensive, I was using others' opinions as proof that my worst fears of unworthiness were true, I asked one of my leaders for some feedback. The division was going through reorganization, and I wanted to gauge what he had in mind for me. I remember in the discussion that he had compared me to another coworker and implied that she was more of a creative thinker and that this was something that I seemed to lack. I felt a sting.

This took me off guard. I felt I was a creative person. I had a couple sets of alarms going off. I had the usual trigger that wanted to use this as proof that I really am not creative and am a fool to ever think I was—the "see, you *are* unworthy" gig. I also had the alarm that said, "You feel defensive; pay attention."

I had to look at the facts. Fact number one was that in this VP's opinion, I was not creative. Why would he think that? And what do other people define as creative thinking? And do I demonstrate this? And as you are probably aware, creativity is a more subjective trait than the color of someone's eyes, and people can express their creativity in different ways and degrees. So I got on Google and looked up "creative thinking" and found a website that had a self-survey that would gauge your creative thinking. I took it and saw that I wasn't high off the charts, but I wasn't down at the bottom either. I had some creative thinking skills.

Then I thought back on my past interactions with the leader and what I'd asked and talked about. I realized that in most of our conversations, I would anxiously ask him repeatedly what his plans were and how I fit in. The uncertainty of the change was having me focus on how I was going to survive, not what I could contribute. I had been in survival mode without realizing it. No wonder he did not see me as a creative thinker.

I no longer felt the sting and had no need to prove to him that I was a creative thinker. I was able look at what was going on in my department that could use some creativity. I looked at how the programs I was accountable for could be improved and expanded in the future and wrote up my thoughts. I focused on what my goals were and took actions toward the type of employee I wanted to be.

The next week, I asked to speak with the VP and thanked him for the feedback. It was because of looking at his perspective and considering what he'd said that I was able to get out of survival mode and refocus on my goals. I felt a renewed sense of engagement and no longer worried about the upcoming changes.

The question to ask is this: *What are you proving and to whom?* Is it really the other person you are trying to convince? If you hadn't perceived this as a threat, would you give the other person some facts as well as get his or her perspective to see why he or she saw things differently?

If I feel it is a threat to what I want and how I want to be viewed, then I feel aggressiveness because of the fear of the other person being right. It is not the fact that he or she has that opinion of me; it is my *fear* that the opinion is accurate. What am I truly afraid of? I am afraid that my fear that I am not good enough is true and that this may be the proof. I am not trying to prove that the other person is wrong for his or her sake; it is for my sake. This whole fight is to protect my own self-image. Yes, I had built up walls of protection, but was it to keep the threat out or to keep the truth in? As it turns out, it was both.

Signs You Are in Survival Mode

So when you are in a fight, it always occurs as a win-lose situation, and you have to win. Your only point of view is that it is the enemy's fault that the situation is so bad, that your life isn't working out, and that you are miserable. But you feel very righteous, so you continue fighting. You spend your time proving that the reason you are unhappy is because of the enemy. If he were just gone, life would be better. Or if she would just do what I want her to do, if she would just admit how wrong she is, I would be able to feel better.

If you really stopped, stepped back, and looked, you would see that you are giving the enemy all the control and then fighting him or her for it.

In Mabel's situation, she went from having a meaningful goal of adding value and being a high performer to putting all her focus on proving that her boss was not being fair and that her reputation needed protection.

What she is not aware of yet is that even if she wins her good fight, she will not get the prize that she wants. She will just be right that it is the enemy's fault that she is not being valued or respected. In the meantime, her behavior will not be consistent with a confident, productive employee.

If she decides to leave the situation as a reaction, she will still not be free, because she will still have a belief about this danger that she has just reinforced as a filter, and her alarm will be set to go off whenever she is in what seems to be a similar situation. And it *will* go off again.

It Is a Vicious Cycle

Watch the news or the latest hit drama or reality show on TV, or listen to conversations around you, and you will become aware that this vicious cycle seems to be the norm. Most of us have picked up the belief that this drama is real life. This is just the way the world works. It is a constant struggle.

There is a lot of agreement that drama is life. We have been sold that the stress of survival is where life really takes place. We humans have gotten so used to being in survival mode that we get suspicious and worried when things are going well and start to prepare for the worst. This becomes a filter, and when something goes wrong, we can yell, "See, I told you it was getting too good!"

We have become paranoid, suspicious, and cynical as our default state of being. Then we can accuse others who are happy and enjoying life of not being real. We forget that the state of survival mode limits what we let through our filters and that we are missing most of what is possible in our lives. Our focus never wavers from proving that it is the enemy's fault that we do not have the lives we want.

These beliefs that we may have picked up from our parents, our culture, or the media will push us to behave in this pattern. It will distract us from the goals that we have created. From pursuing what is meaningful and brings us joy. Some of the beliefs that we may have inherited or acquired are as follows:

- Life is hard.
- You have to look good.

- You have to fit in.
- You have to be perfect.
- You will most likely hate your job.

And so we will go in a direction that we wouldn't choose if we knew we had a choice.

And we are fearful of danger most of the time.

This also has physical effects. Our bodies are not meant to take long periods of the stress that comes with survival mode, yet we have made it the norm. It is taking a toll on our overall health.

You can see now that when we go into survival, when we are in fight-or-flight mode, we don't make progress toward our goals. We actually get off track, and we begin using our time and resources to gather proof as to why we can't have what we want—and, of course, how it is the enemy's fault.

But this is only one side of the coin. This is not all there is or all we have to experience. We are designed to thrive, not just survive. So in the next chapter, we will look at the other option of what life can be. What I believe is meant to be our norm—thriving.

CHAPTER 4

The Game of Thriving and the Joy of Alignment

What if all of life was as fun, exciting, and interesting as the most enjoyable game you ever played? As much fun as a game where you feel focused, creatively deciding your next move, and using the obstacles that occur to improve your skills.

What if life is actually more like that game you love and has you so engaged—celebrating your wins and learning even more from your losses? The game where you are always ready to play another round.

The only thing that differentiates our play from real life is the definition we give for each, and therefore the beliefs we have around games vs. real life. Nothing more. There is nothing more valid about what we define as going to work than there is about what we call play except for what we have been taught or choose to believe.

There is a belief we have been given that if you are playing or having fun, then you are being lazy and unproductive. Accomplishments are not considered real or impactful unless you have experienced some distress or pain in reaching them, having to pay your dues. We have heard "No pain, no gain." Our brains translate this into never being able to gain, or call it gain, without pain. We have been told this again and again by our parents, teachers, and bosses. Somehow, we never question this wisdom, but deep down we know it isn't how we would have designed things.

As we discussed earlier, our belief is the filter our unconscious brain uses to decide what we see, do, and experience. So if we believe life and work are meant to be hard, our experiences match up, and we are left feeling stressed, unfulfilled, and constricted in our real life.

In her book *Reality Is Broken,* game designer Jane McGonigal talks about how we have defined games as fun but not serious (McGonigal, 2011). Reality, on the other hand, is serious by American culture's definition. This could be one of the reasons being in survival mode has become the norm for so many. We want to be in reality, so we believe we need to be serious—in our attitudes, our actions, and even our facial expressions—grave in our approach to what matters to us. This may be rooted in many things, even a wish to erase our childhood or negative actions taken as a youth. It may be as simple as adults who constantly said, "Grow up!" or "Be serious!" when we thought we were just having fun.

Who says?

What if being serious about everything in order to be real, adult, or mature is just a belief that we inherited or acquired along with everyone else? What if we are all wondering why it has to be this way and yet are afraid to ask the question?

What if life is meant to be fun, and we could approach everything we experience in our day-to-day activity in the same spirit as playing our favorite game with our friends?

What if we are more productive when we are feeling happy, excited, and engaged rather than worried, pressured, and stressed out?

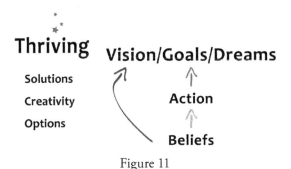

Figure 11

Actually, studies of the brain have found evidence that this is likely the case. We are more productive and creative, make more innovative connections of information, and learn more quickly when we are engaged and feel a sense of freedom than when we are stressed or feel threatened.

What if life was fun? What if we are designed to thrive? I believe we are.

Take my sister, Helen, who started her own business in 2012, a tutoring center franchise. Up until then, she had a very successful career as a director in a large corporation where she worked for twenty-seven years. She was very knowledgeable in her area and loved managing and developing the people under her.

But her dream was to own a tutoring center.

In the first year and a half of her center's existence, she has never considered it a struggle. Her focus is continuously on the main goal of making a difference for as many kids as possible. She creates goals or little games along the way for the growth of her business, such as projecting the number of students or tutors she would like to have each month.

You can tell she is thriving by the things that she talks about. When she calls me up, it is to tell me the cool thing that happened that day—what a parent had said, how a person called asking if she could be a tutor at exactly the time that Helen needed a tutor, or how the center just reached a new attendance goal. The only other reason Helen calls is to tell me her next awesome idea, her "wouldn't it be great if ..." And she is always coming up with great ideas. She has the room to be creative and innovative because she is imagining a future she prefers instead of worrying about what could go wrong. And when someone tells her "that can't be done," making whatever they believe is impossible becomes part of her fun.

Helen is thriving.

And it permeates her whole life, her strong marriage and relationship with her family, her love of playing tennis and her health. People wonder how things seem to flow and work smoothly for her.

She is creating the experience as a game: a meaningful, mindful game.

A life of thriving is a life that has us feel free to grow and learn, to move toward the goals that we see are meaningful, and actually have fun along the way. There are many similarities to how we feel when we are at play and when we are thriving.

To thrive, we need to change our filter. Instead of a filter of fear, warning us that the people around us are our enemies, that we are surrounded by tigers, we can instead use a filter of an enjoyable game, inviting us to play.

This may have some of you saying, but wait, if we stopped looking for those tigers, won't we get blindsided by people who are out to take advantage of others? Valid question, but thriving and being focused on what we want instead of looking for all the danger does not mean being blind or naïve, quite the opposite. It has us seeing more of what is truly happening and positions us to make better decisions.

In an interview with Nigel Warburton, English illusionist and mentalist, Derren Brown states, "Somewhat counterintuitively, it's the more trusting people that actually emerge as less gullible (Open University, 2010). They obviously get fooled, as we all do … but they tend to be very good at learning from those experiences where they have been duped, they tend not to generalize it over everybody and then become cynical about everything, which makes them more effective socially."

When we are thriving, focused on what we want and not being paranoid, we are more open to learning, connecting information, which has us become more effective in all situations.

We have talked about what the focus and behaviors are when we are in survival mode; now let's look at the focus and behaviors of thriving mode.

Creating a Mindful Game

Buckminster Fuller said, "You never change things by fighting the existing reality. To change something, build a new model that makes the existing model obsolete."

As I have just described in the last chapter, most of us have been living in a model of life that has being in survival mode predominate, and we are ready to have this reality change. To do this, we don't want to fight the "existing reality," as Fuller stated, but to create a new model, one where thriving is our natural way of being.

The thriving side of the Thriving beyond Survival model gives an alternative to the dramatic and stressful villain, victim, and hero scenario and instead gives us an opportunity to look at life as a mindful game.

Building and then living in a new model is simpler than you may think, though it will take some effort and discipline. For most of us, when we hear effort and discipline, we picture a scenario like school or a gym where we are making ourselves do something that we really don't enjoy because either we believe it will be good for us or because we know the teacher or coach is watching. There is an element of drudgery and resistance that sometimes gets connected to effort and discipline.

Thriving is about enjoying our growth and experiences. So when it comes to thriving, effort and discipline does not mean exhaustion and punishment; those belong in the old model of drama. The effort and discipline will come in the form of being mindful.

What is Mindfulness?

Being mindful is being in the present moment and observing what we are feeling, thinking, and believing in that moment from the point of view of an observer while still being a participant. I have found that most of the time, especially when we have been triggered into survival mode, we are not experiencing what is actually happening now as much as we are remembering and reliving something similar that happened in the past, and we find the situation and emotions uncomfortably familiar. Or we are picturing a future that is ironically similar and worse than the situations we have experienced in the past and have programmed our filter to help us avoid.

Unfortunately, it is quite possible to struggle for an entire lifetime without ever truly thriving in the present moment. What people typically do is to take the past and push it into the future, either as a comfortable status quo or as a danger to be avoided or overcome. This prevents us from ever really dealing with the present moment, of taking that spark of life and creating our own story. It doesn't have to be this way.

Being mindful allows us to be aware of these habits of thought and reactions that we follow automatically so that we can choose different thoughts, beliefs, and actions that create the possibility of more outcomes that we prefer. We can choose to practice inside of a new model.

Choosing to do something new is a bold step but one we can look at with joy and not fear. Creating a new order of things requires only that we begin to see things differently. It only appears frightening because we haven't tried it yet. On the other side of our new achievement, it appears to light the way for more triumphs. As Pema Chodron has said, "Fear is a natural reaction of moving closer to the truth."

Being mindful is a skill we are all capable of and have used. Think about any new skill that you have ever learned. It took focused attention. If you learn to play the guitar, you have to focus on where you put your fingers on the strings, how it feels to press them down, and what the correct sound of the chord is to know if you are on track. When we are being aware, our brain is open to learning and creating new connections and pathways that will create new ways to think and behave.

When reacting automatically or doing anything by habit, the brain is actually fairly quiet and doesn't make any new connections; it does not learn. There are no new thoughts, ideas, or choices available. So nothing new is done or learned when we are not paying attention and are reliving our stories of the past or fearing the future. And this adds to our feelings of being stuck. A way to get out of automatic is to be mindful.

You can build your skill of mindfulness by checking in with how you are feeling both physically and emotionally during your day and acknowledging moments when you are fully aware of what you are experiencing.

If you have not thought about consciously paying attention and being like this before, start now—this moment. Notice how you are positioned as you read this book. Where are your feet and arms? Are you feeling relaxed, or do you feel tension anywhere in your body? What are the thoughts, opinions, or judgments you are making about this activity? Listen to them as if you were listening to someone else say them. Listen so that you can observe yourself hearing what your thoughts are saying.

This simple activity has you inside and outside of the experience at the same time. It enables you to consciously focus on what you do or think next, and when you have that focus, you can consciously make a choice. You have the ability to consciously decide what thought you want to think next. And the more you practice this awareness when you are feeling safe, the more your brain is learning to be mindful. The more you practice, the more consistent you will become, and though consciously choosing will always take effort (it is the opposite of automatically responding), the less effort it will feel like it takes to pay attention.

Your awareness will grow not just in the quiet times but in those times when you have negative emotions. And it is then that you will have the most powerful opportunity to be conscious of choosing.

Meditation is also a very effective way to build the skill of awareness in a conscious and consistent manner. There are many ways to meditate. If learning or practicing meditation appeals to you, I encourage you to explore which method works best for you for calming your mind and giving you a safe way to build this skill. Many studies have found that just fifteen minutes a day of meditation can have many beneficial results (Blue, 2012).

The Mindful Game

Now that we understand the mindful part of a mindful game of thriving, let's look at how we can bring in the concepts of a game.

Games can be complex or simple, intricate or straightforward, brief, long-term, or even take years to complete. According to game designer Jane McGonigal, every game has four elements: the object of the game, unnecessary obstacles, feedback, and the ability to opt in. (McGonigal, 2011).

Element 1: The Object of the Game

The first element is that all games have a goal, the object of the game. Just like with our lives and in the Thriving beyond Survival model, the goal is what we use to focus, to measure progress, and to determine success; it's how you know what success is for you.

We all have our goals, including the goals that we created at the beginning of this book. Our goals determine what success is, what winning will uniquely look like for each of us.

Beliefs drive your action in thriving as much as they do in survival. When you have a goal that you believe is worthwhile, that is meaningful and is something that you want to accomplish, it is easy to move into action. When you believe the goal is possible, even if you don't know exactly how you will accomplish it, you are still excited to get started. There is a sense of anticipation and even joy. You feel a determination that allows you to be persistent and allows you to learn and grow.

Your positive beliefs will filter information and opportunities to your conscious brain. And just like in the story of the blue cars, when we are in thriving mode, not feeling threatened by the feedback we receive, we can see our beliefs as a choice that allows us to be open to different perspectives and solutions. We know that they can be adjusted through experience and the gathering of more information; they can grow as we grow.

Remember these words: "When you have a goal that you *believe* is worthwhile ..." Recall that it is your beliefs that drive your actions.

When you are focused on your goal, your filter looks for options and opportunities that will enable you to progress. When you have a vision of what success is, that is when your brain gets creative.

Our unconscious and conscious mind will make connections, form ideas, and seek out answers from all the data that is coming toward us. Instead of looking for danger, it is seeking solutions. This feeling of focus and creativity and joy has also been called *being in the flow* or *being in the zone*.

Now our filter is broadened and open to seeing opportunities and options. It will look for the answer to the questions we are asking. So if you believe that you are going to find a way to accomplish a goal, your brain will look for information that will help you. It is part of the creativity that all humans are born with, the ability to find new ways of doing things, improving our skills, of learning.

My sister, Helen, had never owned a business before opening her tutoring center and knew little about marketing, accounting, operations, and other skills that it takes to run a business, but because she was focused on her goal, she didn't let the lack of knowledge or skill stop her. She learned what she needed and found others who were able to provide expertise.

Let's recall the example of Brandi Carlile, another person able to thrive. She appears to have found her mindful game and is playing it successfully. Her goals, on and off stage, are aligned. She is enjoying her life and sharing that joy with others. There are other people you may know in your own life who seem to live that magical fairytale, whose goals seem to fall into place. The moment I realized what I loved to do and was good at—training and developing myself and others—amazing things started to happen in my life. The last few jobs I had fell in my lap. I find I am able to talk to people about what I do and to naturally and organically connect to the right people.

And the right opportunities have opened up in other aspects of my life that are important to me. Music is essential to my life. When I decided to learn to play drums, within three months, my drum instructor presented me with an opportunity to join a band in need of a drummer. The band is made up of four other talented and amazing human beings. We are good friends and collaborate well together—and are having tons of fun. We have played at local venues, been on national cable television, recorded a CD, and have been in contention for a Grammy. These events are beyond any I would have ever imagined.

I am no different in this ability to have an amazing life than Brandi Carlile or you. And I find that when I keep dreaming, new and exciting things keep happening. When I keep choosing to thrive, I thrive.

Element 2: Unnecessary Obstacles

When you are invited to play a new game, and after you have found out what the object of the game is, the next thing you want to know is how to play—what the rules are for this game. What are the obstacles that need to be overcome?

When playing tennis, you have to hit a ball of a certain size with a racket over a net, and get it within certain lines on the ground of specific dimensions. These rules of the game of tennis are the context that makes the game unique. And it is because of these otherwise unnecessary obstacles that we see a game as play, as fun.

Thriving
Solutions
Creativity
Options
Opponents/Obstacles
Respect

These obstacles are important; they not only distinguish the game but also inform our skills and our strategies for winning.

In life as well as any game, we also need to know the rules in order to reach our goal. Whether they are processes, laws, policies, or even a matter of location, it is by successfully navigating the obstacles and using the rules that we are able to know what skills to improve, be creative, feel challenged, and learn.

When in thriving mode, it is our focus and beliefs that have something look like an interesting obstacle rather than a barrier that we use to prove that we can't have what we want or prefer. I know that when I am working on a project that is meaningful to me and I enjoy, like creating a workshop, I am thriving. I am having fun not only in the delivering of the event but the creation too. I still run into obstacles such as delay in the printing, the room not being set up right, or technical difficulties with the computers, and though I may have an initial feeling of "ugh" like you do when you miss a shot in tennis, it is easy to get refocused on the overall goal of an effective session and find ways around the obstacles. It is where I apply more of my innovation and creativity and get to shine. Because I am focused on my goal, I am not looking for a tiger to blame or berate.

Obstacles as Part of the Fun

When we get better at playing a game, when we have increased our skill so that what used to be a challenge is now easy, we look for ways to make the game a little harder to test and build our skills. And just like in a game, when our day-to-day obstacles become too easy, we want a new challenge that lets us test and build our skills.

When we are in thriving mode, we are able to view the obstacles we encounter on the way to our goal in a similar way as we would the obstacles in a game. It becomes fun! Our brain is hungry for new things because it is designed to learn. Obstacles ensure we have that opportunity.

Mabel experienced being in thriving mode in the past, though she was unaware of how she got there. When Mabel was in this mode, her primary goal was being highly productive and efficient. She found it easy to focus on her work, and she liked it when her coworkers brought her a challenging issue, because she really enjoyed figuring out the solution. She loved the feeling of contributing to her team.

Who Else Is Playing the Game?

You may recall that in our vision of creating life exactly as we wanted it, one of the questions was "Who else is there?" Chances are you are not playing this game by yourself. There may be others who are going for the same vision as you, who believe in the goal, and you are cooperating and collaborating toward success. We will look at teammates in a moment. But first let's look at who else may be playing the game.

In many games, you have an opponent, a fellow participant who brings in an extra level of interest and unpredictability. Because we are viewing this as a game, this adds to the challenge and fun. We respect the role the opponent plays.

When pursuing a goal while being in the flow and thriving, not everyone will agree with us or want the same things that we do. But when thriving, we don't see these people as enemies that we then need to focus on defeating. Just like in a game, we see them as opponents, and we value the role they play.

When you play a game with an opponent, do you want to play only with someone who you can beat every time? That would get boring. You want someone who will challenge you and cause you to hone your skills and find new ways to look at things.

You may have played a game in which the competition between you and your opponent was very intense, both of you going for that goal, the win. And at the end of the game, even if you lost, you maintained respect for the other player. Because of a strong opponent, you may even have played better than you ever had before and learned a new perspective.

When you are in thriving mode, you respect those who have a different perspective or viewpoint. You may not agree with them, and you may have some intense interactions, but the focus is on looking for ways to reach your goal. And if they are saying no or have a different opinion, you want to know why.

Even if you don't agree with someone, having their perspective gives you more information and can lead to the creation of more ideas or solutions.

If you recall that the most data points that our consciousness can see at any moment is forty out of eleven million, someone who does not agree with you may have a set of forty different data points that may be valuable for you to know. If you choose to believe that someone who does not agree with you may be a source of new information, you can react with curiosity rather than needing to prove that your point of view is right.

Your focus remains staying on track with your goal. You get curious as to what your opponent's goal may be, so you ask questions to see if there is a way that you both can reach your objectives. There is an ease and flow even with the intensity. And again, we have a sense of fun when we are in this mode, when we are focused on our goal.

If you have respect for your opponents, you are not seeing them as enemies. And they are not your main focus but simply an interesting part of the game. You may not agree with them, you may not even like them, but you are able to respect them. You can listen to them in a way you can't when they are the enemy. You look for ways that you both may be able to win. Or you look for ways to get around them as you would an obstacle. You don't need them as proof that you can't have what you want; they are instrumental in honing your skills or clarifying the path to your goal. They may give you information that allows you to strategize how to overcome other potential obstacles.

Through it all, the focus is not on beating your opponent; it is on reaching your goal.

Many of the biggest rivalries in sports were respected friends off the field or court. Martina Navratilova and Chris Evert in tennis, Larry Bird and Magic Johnson in basketball, Arnold Palmer and Jack Nicklaus in golf, and most recently snowboarders Shaun White and Iouri Podladtchikov are all considered some of the top sport rivalries of all time. With each pair, there was great respect and friendship despite the role they played in the game. These players appreciated the other's skill and contribution to their own growth in their game. When Iouri Podladtchikov dethroned Shaun White to win the gold in the half-pipe competition at the Sochi Olympic games, he immediately bear-hugged the snowboarding legend and said thanks.

Teammates

Others who may be in the game are those you see as teammates, going toward the same goal because it aligns with their personal desires and brings them meaning.

As we have discussed, unconscious beliefs are thoughts that we have turned into a truth about reality. And because our filter is set to show us what we are looking for, we find proof that reinforces our beliefs. This works for both beneficial and unbeneficial beliefs.

Another reinforcement of beliefs that makes them seem even more like the truth is when we have agreement from others. When we believe that we are not worthy, or a teacher tells us we will never amount to anything, our belief has been reinforced. When we are telling people about how bad things are, like Mabel was doing, we are looking for that agreement so that we are reassured that our belief is not a belief but truth, and so that we feel justified in wanting to annihilate our perceived enemy.

Agreement also reinforces beliefs we have that are beneficial. When we believe we are good at a skill, and someone acknowledges us for it, we feel good, and it reinforces that belief too. This is why recognition of what we are doing that is working helps motivate us to repeat behaviors that move us toward our goal.

Agreement becomes a big element when working with others, when part of a team. Agreement of beliefs with a group, whether conscious or unconscious, is what creates that group's culture. It is what forms the rules for their interaction. It creates a group of people aligned with each other. And just as with individuals, if the belief is beneficial, it helps them progress toward their goal as a group. If the belief is unbeneficial, it will keep them in survival mode. If a group of employees believe that they are not listened to, they will not only have the proof through their filters but a lot of agreement from the others in the group. And if someone doesn't agree, they become the enemy, and drama ensues. Meanwhile, the group's goals and the individual's goals are put aside in order to fight the good fight. Yet they are supposedly on the same team.

Agreement is not a bad thing at all. It is actually what allows us to operate and flow as individuals in a group. There is an agreement that red streetlights mean stop and green ones mean go. This agreement is widespread, and most of us stop at red without much thought. Red does not inherently mean stop, but we agreed to let it mean that. The same goes with the days of the week. There is really nothing real about Monday except that we have agreed on it. And my believing that today is Monday along with everyone else is not infringing on what I want for myself or my goals. It is part of the rules of the game in the society I am in at the moment, and so I accept it with no issue. There wasn't always a Monday, and there are even still some cultures and tribes that have no concept of it being Monday. When we join a group, knowing that the rules or beliefs of the culture or society are created and not necessarily the truth allows for more of a sense of play and choice in our behavior. This agreement enables things to work smoothly, not only for us but those around us.

Cultural Beliefs

Cultures and societies have picked up certain beliefs that they filter for and find agreement with; these beliefs do not always line up with what they want or align with the best interests of all the individuals. However, because there is agreement that it is the truth, it remains so until enough people are willing to agree with a more beneficial belief. Take the earlier example of "no pain, no gain." Is this really true? Can people only grow stronger and wiser through pain? Pain may instruct, but is it the only and most effective instructor? Tearing down muscle does cause the body to need to rebuild, and consequently it will make itself stronger, but is this the only way to grow stronger? Is the strength being built because it is good for the body or is it being built because there is a belief that this strength is what will enable someone to be accepted (because of having experienced and overcome pain)?

Is it true that there is no gain without pain, or is it just a phrase that enough people said over and over to reinforce the belief into a truth? Is it merely an axiom that causes people to behave in ways that cause them pain because they think that is the only way to grow?

Once you begin examining some of these familiar beliefs, you may come up with your own questions.

Buckminster Fuller was at a juncture in his life where he saw that he wasn't winning in society's game. He had flunked out of Harvard twice, lost backers' money in his business ventures, and endured the loss of a child. He was at rock bottom when he decided that instead of suicide he was going to use his life as an experiment. Instead of buying into society's game of needing to earn a living and so having to put all his focus on making money, he would focus on looking for what would make things better in the world in any way he was able, and through this, he believed, he would be supported by the universe. He would see what one average, healthy individual could do. He began to play a different game; the rules to this new game included that "questions … must be answered only in terms of experience … Hearsaids, beliefs, axioms, superstitions, guesses, opinions were and are all excluded as (my) answer resources." His game was based on the premise that we each have a reason for being here that benefits the universe, or we would not exist, and he looked for agreement within his experience rather than with what everyone else believed.

As a result of disciplining himself to think for himself and experimenting with what he saw could benefit everyone, he contributed a lot to architecture, system theory, design, science, and how we as humans can look at purpose here on earth. He demonstrates an alternative game to play. He didn't go into survival mode and try to prove that the current society was wrong. He looked at an outcome for the world that he preferred. Instead of us against them, based on lack, he chose to approach life based on the knowledge that the earth has enough resources to support everyone. He felt we just had to discover them and take action consistent with that. He played a mindful game of thriving.

In our game of thriving, we are able to think for ourselves and be conscious of that to which we give our agreement. Are we in agreement with the values both stated and practiced by the team we are on, and do they align with our own values? Do we agree with what the team believes is important, possible, and meaningful? Do we agree with the limitations or complaints that the group has? We see that we have a choice that not only makes a difference for our personal experience but influences the rest of the team.

Here is a suggestion for you. In your conversations today, listen to what your discussions are mostly about. Are you looking for a solution or explaining and justifying a problem? Are you looking for agreement for how great something is or looking for agreement on how bad something is? Then consciously choose what you would rather have the conversation be about and talk about that.

Element 3: Feedback

"What's the score of the game?"

Every good game has a way to give feedback to constantly let us know how we are doing in the game. It's a way to keep track of how we are progressing.

A basketball player knows how she is doing not only by the score of the game but her percentage of completed baskets. With this feedback, she is able to make any adjustments she needs to keep on track to win. Note that the score is not innately negative or positive; it is simply an indicator that lets her know how to adjust. She may not like it at the moment, but it gives her the information she needs to make changes, learn, and grow in order to progress.

In pursuit of our own goals, we crave the data, the feedback that gives us information on our progress. When we are thriving, we don't necessarily see feedback as positive or negative; we see it as essential because it allows us to adjust and learn. And much of our learning will occur subconsciously if we are open and focused on what we want to achieve. Every mistake becomes an opportunity to gain new information that we are then able to use to keep going in our chosen direction.

Organisms thrive on feedback. It lets you know if the actions you are taking are on course toward your goal and gives you the opportunity to adjust your actions and behaviors to keep on track.

When you are in thriving mode, you welcome any and all feedback. You are able to hear what may be considered criticism as good information. Because you are not using it as proof that you can't achieve your goal, you are seeing it as information that allows you to adjust. You are able to be persistent.

Thriving
Solutions
Creativity
Options
Opponents/Obstacles
Respect
Persistence

Again, it is not whether you like it or not. You may not like the information, but you see it as useful. You are also able to sort out people's perspectives, their beliefs, from the data that they filtered and their interpretation to fit their story. You are able to get to the useful facts and not to have others' opinions and judgments stop you or become proof that you can't have what you want.

Therefore, when we are in thriving, a no does not become proof that we can't have what we want; we are not afraid to be persistent, to keep going and asking for more information.

A failure or mistake doesn't stop us either.

Persistence

When I play Angry Birds on my smartphone, it has me hurtling little birds with certain abilities toward a structure hiding the mean green piggies. If I get them all, I can go to the next level. And I get a certain number of points that will give me one to three stars for my effort. I always want to get three stars. So I will play a level until I have gotten the points to earn the third star. I fail many times, but the failure doesn't make me feel bad. With each failure, I learn something new. And I see my average consistently get higher until I finally get the required score.

When we incorporate failure as part of our learning to get us closer to the goal, we stay persistent. We see setbacks as a way to expand and grow. They become interesting, and they challenge our skill. We get to be creative deciding what to do next time.

I take drum lessons, and I rely on my instructor, Jeff, to give me feedback. Because I am using all four limbs of my body in ways that are new, it is hard for me to keep track of everything at once. I may be getting both my hands to do what I want but have no idea that my feet are putting in an extra beat. The only way I can adjust is to have it brought to my attention. When tutoring children in math skills, it is important to know what problems they are getting wrong in order to know what explanation may increase their understanding. And when my nephew started experimenting with growing lettuce and spinach using hydroponics, it was when the plants were dying that he learned what the best indoor light source needed to be. All of these are examples of how valuable failures are to our learning. When we are thriving, the feedback is welcomed as a sign that we are moving into new, more challenging territory.

Element 4: Opt In

The final element and the most important that makes a game a game is the ability to opt in. When someone opts in to a game, they are willing to play within the rules of the game, confront the opponents, and strategize around obstacles, all as part of the fun.

It's about having a meaningful goal that we believe in, that we believe is worth pursuing and that we know we can make happen. When our beliefs and goals are aligned, and we take essential actions, we have opted in. This is when we are at our best, when we are thriving.

Like my sister, Helen, with her new business and Brandi with her music, we are having fun on the path to our goal. We are not waiting until we have accomplished the goal to be happy. We delight in our forward progress. We are engaged in our journey toward the goal; we are engaged in life.

Engagement is not only an indicator that we are working at our optimum level, but it also helps us to broaden and build our ability to reproduce optimum performance.

When you are hired for a job, you in essence have opted into your understanding of the goals, expectations, and policies that the role requires. You are excited about what you can learn, accomplish, and contribute. You are in thriving mode.

Because of the opt-in feature of all games, we have a choice. In any situation, we have a choice to move toward what we want and thrive or to go into survival mode. We choose what we focus on, how we filter and interpret data, and the actions that we take.

Always.

It is not about choosing not to ever feel fear or any other negative emotion; it is about choosing how we respond when those emotions are felt.

When you opt into a game, the rules and obstacles create the fun instead of making the activity a chore, drudgery, or work.

Opting in is a matter of framing, how you are seeing and approaching the situation. Your perspective.

Why is opting in so important?

Opting in acknowledges that you have a choice and that you are choosing to set and achieve the goal you have created or have been given. There is an implication of autonomy and the ability to have a say in what you are doing. This is what makes you as a human different from an object or a machine—the ability to choose based on your own perspective.

Opting into a game means that you have accepted the goal of the game, the rules and expectations of how the game will be played, and how success is measured. The constraints are the unnecessary obstacles that distinguish this particular game. When you opt in, you are ready to play, to figure out how to reach your goals within the rules of the game, and develop new skills and strategies to overcome its particular obstacles and achieve success. This is what allows us to have fun and find joy in the progress toward our goal.

Thriving
Solutions
Creativity
Options
Opponents/Obstacles
Respect
Joy/Fun

To someone watching you play your game, the rules and obstacles you face to reach the goal may seem ridiculous (you can't tell me hitting little piggies with birds is not ridiculous or hitting a ball into a hole in the ground for that matter). But to you and the others playing, there is meaning. It is this sense of meaning that makes opting into the game so important.

A pioneer in positive psychology, Martin Seligman has defined happiness as pleasure, engagement, and meaning. His studies have confirmed that people who pursue all three routes lead the fullest lives. Meaning is a prime motivator in keeping you in action. If you do not feel or believe that what you are doing has any meaning, you will either feel suffering or stop.

The interesting thing is that we are the ones that determine what is meaningful for us. If what matters to me is expressing my creativity, or using my analytical skills to look for patterns, or some other strength, this gives the tasks I am doing meaning for me. It is aligned with my overall goal for myself and part of my mindful game of thriving.

What many of us also find meaningful is doing a task that means something for others, even if it brings no direct value to us. If you agree or opt in to do something at the request of someone else, for instance to help someone move, its meaning is clearly bound up in the value it has for that other person. If we know that what we do makes a difference to our customer, our neighbor, or our community, it adds meaning for us.

On the other hand, if we believe that the task that we are doing for someone else really doesn't mean anything to him or her, then we feel the task as work. If we can, we stop. And if we feel we can't stop, we disengage, we withdraw, and suddenly we are in survival mode.

A study by behavioral economist and researcher Dan Ariely showed that even when getting paid for a task, people would choose to stop sooner if they felt it was meaningless (Ariely, 2012).

What If the Rules Unexpectedly Change?

Here are some things, then, to keep in mind when you are playing a mindful game of thriving. There may be times when you opt into a job or role and the rules change. You may be given goals that you would not have chosen for yourself. Or, perhaps you are involved in a reorganization in your company that changes your original role or department. There are other roles that may bring changes, such as being a child of aging parents, having children, purchasing and managing a home, etc. When they become difficult and unpredictable, these are situations where many people tend to disengage or feel trapped.

This reaction is valid and understandable. When you are told you have a new role or goal, and you believe you have no choice or ability to opt in, you may feel that your autonomy, one of your main intrinsic motivators, is being threatened. It may feel like you are no longer seen as a human individual but as an object or machine needed to do whatever the leaders or the family want, or that you are in a situation that you have no choice or ability to leave. You may find yourself in survival mode, falling into fight/flight, searching for supporters of your side, fighting the good fight, and feeling totally justified. The problem is that you feel miserable and stuck the whole time.

Making any decision in the mode of survival will usually be about fight or flight. And if you stay and fight, you will make only slow progress. You will feel the stress of the work it takes to prove that you are right—but only about them being wrong by keeping you from what you want.

If you decide to flee, to leave while in survival mode, you will take the same belief and fear with you that you can't have or don't deserve what you want. You will bundle more proof and evidence and roll it up into your truth. This choice will increase the probability that you will find similar issues coming up in whatever next job or role you take.

Now let us look at thriving again. When you are in thriving mode, the decision to opt in or out of the current situation can be made based on how well your personal goals align with the opportunities around you. When you are making a decision in thriving mode, the focus is on the goals that are important to you and not about sticking it out because you have no choice, or leaving with bitterness and resentment with the other people in the situation.

In the last years of his life, my dad had frontal temporal dementia. This type of dementia affected his ability to communicate so that his behavior was unpredictable. He was unable to verbalize nouns, so it was hard to know what he wanted, and he needed to have someone with him at all times. This was emotionally exhausting, especially for my mom. Often she would bring him by on the weekends for me to watch him while she got errands done.

Before I had the distinctions of the model, I was often in survival mode with the condition my dad had and the belief that my mom was just using me as a babysitter and that she should have been better at taking care of him. I felt powerlessness, resentment, sadness, and anger.

This situation was not fair. I did not want my dad to have dementia and was angry that this was happening to such a gentle and intelligent man. It was easy to have negative emotions around this situation, and with those came a need for an enemy, a tiger to fight. The disease and my mom were easy targets.

When I saw the success in changing how I reacted to situations at work and how much easier it became to deal with the stress there, I decided to make an effort to have the same success in this situation. I created a goal that I would make every moment with my dad special no matter what was happening or how he was behaving. I changed my focus when I was with him to being about spending the time I had with him, knowing it was short. I opted into a meaningful and mindful game.

There may be times when you find that you are in a position or role in which you can't leave or opt out for certain reasons.

When you create your own goal, it feels easier to opt in. The same choice of opting in is available, even if you are in a position you don't want or you are not interested in the goals you have been given. Opting in will keep or bring you back to thriving mode.

How do you do this? First, get clarity on how this goal fits into the bigger picture and see if that bigger picture is one that you can align with and opt into. Get facts and data on the expectations of what success is in the situation so that you know the rules to this game. And if you are still not in a place that you feel you want to opt into, create your own vision of the goal and what you can accomplish that will be meaningful for you.

I found myself needing to practice this strategy a few years ago when I found my role at work was changing in a direction that I would not have chosen.

Here is how it went:

My heart sinks when I read the spreadsheet from my director, containing my goals for the upcoming year.

"What is going on?" I groan to myself.

Last year, I loved my job. I worked on projects that I couldn't believe I was getting paid to do. My performance review from my manager was good, and I received glowing feedback from others in the organization. So today I am stunned to realize that none of that work is on my new goal list. I feel like someone just poured gasoline on my hot-fudge sundae.

There are times when you have to deal with unforeseen changes in your role or circumstance. This could be a change in anything from your work projects to dealing with a new baby or family member who has suddenly taken ill and needs special care. These are not changes you like or would have chosen for yourself, yet they are important responsibilities that you need to handle.

When things feel out of our control, our sense of autonomy is threatened, and this puts us into a state of survival, which increases our stress and becomes a distraction from what we really want for ourselves. The experience becomes drudgery. We complain to ourselves and others, and we resent the day-to-day tasks we now have to do. We disengage. And in essence, we abdicate any of our autonomy or power, waiting for the leader to reengage us.

In my circumstance, I did not have control over the new goals I was given. Signing up for the job meant that as long as I continued to work there, I did what my manager needed me to do.

What I did have control over was my perspective and the next actions I took. I decided that my thriving was more important to me than going into that downward spiral of indignation, misery, and disengagement. And to wait for my leader to reengage me seemed to be just further giving up my sense of autonomy.

Here are some of the things I did differently that saved my sanity.

First, I created a personal vision for myself, which gave me something to focus on. My vision was to make a difference for my department and the clients I worked with.

I then had a conversation with my manager, asking for information to get context and clarity on how this change contributed to the overall goal of the organization. I also voiced how I felt about the change, what I saw as my strengths, and what it was that I had enjoyed about my previous role. This allowed me to advocate for myself and feel heard so that I could move forward.

Next, I looked for and found ways that the new goal aligned with my personal vision of making a difference and began taking action.

It took some effort, but I was then able to engage and bring my strengths and creativity to the new role I was given. The amount of stress I felt about the situation decreased significantly, and I was able to get myself back to a place I could thrive.

When we feel our autonomy is threatened, it is not our control that has been taken away, but our *sense* of control. Our autonomy comes from our ability to choose how we respond to a situation, not our ability to always have the circumstances line up as we planned. When things go a way we don't particularly like or wouldn't have chosen ourselves, disengaging or fighting back never really has us feel more in control because the response is a reaction to the belief that control has been taken away. This reaction just reinforces our fear that we have no control because we are usually blaming someone for how wrong things have gone and how unfair it is, so we trap ourselves. We forget that keeping our focus on our primary goal and progressing forward is where our autonomy and power lie.

Here are some questions to get you started:

- What is my personal vision/goal?
- What is the big picture of this new situation?
- What do I need to communicate to feel heard?
- Can I align the goal of this new situation with my personal vision?
- What is the next best action?

The Option of Opting Out

On the other hand, staying in a game that is not using your strengths or aligned with what you want, simply because you believe that it is a bad thing to quit, may keep you stuck and in a continuously stressful situation. Watch for beliefs like "never quit" that are absolutes and have no flexibility when circumstances change. "Never give up" was admirable when Churchill said it during World War II. You may be in a situation with much less at stake for you to take another direction.

The Risk Taker

I had never thought about myself as a risk taker. And before that day, I don't think others did either. I was the quiet, reasonable one. This day, I had just finished attending a seminar for work in California and was spending time with my sister Ginny who was living there. We were halfway through the movie when the reality of what I had done just a few hours before hit me full in the gut.

What am I going to do? I thought.

I took in a deep breath as the drama on the screen faded and the drama of my life filled my thoughts. I looked around at the people seated next me. The stranger on my right, slumped in her seat and totally engrossed, Ginny on my left, who gave me a concerned glance and then quickly got back into the story on the screen. I replayed the earlier conversation on my own private screen.

"So how is the seminar going?" Darlene, my coworker and friend, asked.

"It's good. I have learned a lot and met some really interesting people and ..." I hesitated and took a deep breath, and then I jumped. "I think I have come to a decision. I'm resigning."

"What? Did you find another job?" Darlene asked with a mixture of shock and a hint of envy.

When I stated I had not even started to look for a job, her mood went from shock to concern and worry. That was the reaction that I would get from almost everyone I told I was quitting my job with no other job lined up to step into, especially my mother.

Most people would never just quit their jobs. It just isn't prudent to up and quit the security of a job, even one that's wearing you down. "You should at least have an offer," they'd say. Before this day, I may have agreed with them. I had not left my former job of seven years without having the one I was now leaving lined up. What was different now? What made me just take the leap?

Many times we find ourselves in a situation that we don't like, often our jobs. We feel stifled and unfulfilled, wanting something more. But somewhere along the way, we picked up the belief that this is just the way life goes. Everyone hates Mondays, but you have a job, so just deal with it, suck it up, and be grateful. That feeling of being resigned to misery so that we can feel secure just gets us stuck. We don't feel engaged in our jobs, and we lose the magic of dreaming.

On this day, the day I quit, I was at that point of full realization that the job I was in was not a fit. It was wearing me down, and I was not using my strengths. I liked my coworkers, believed in the company, and was told my performance was good, all reasons to stay; however, doing the duties of the job was drudgery. I could have done what most people do, stick around and go through the motions, start a search, all the while feeling stressed and overwhelmed.

What was different on this day was that I didn't view the decision as whether to leave my job or stay; I viewed it as deciding to find something that would make me happy, that was a fit for me.

I chose me.

When I thought about it like that, it didn't seem like a risk at all. It felt like freedom.

Appreciation

As the Thriving beyond Survival model makes clear, you have a choice in how you react to your emotions. You have the ability to opt into a game that you are not ready to leave yet. You have control over your own engagement.

How can you recognize that control and increase your engagement? One of the distinguishing and powerful emotions of thriving is that of appreciation.

Figure 12

We know we are in thriving mode when we have true appreciation for the situation, the people we are working with, and, most importantly, ourselves. We are focusing on what we want to have happen.

When we are focusing on our goals and what we appreciate, it programs our filters to find more options, and signs of growth, and progress.

There can be intensity in our pursuit, but the focus is always on accomplishing our goal. The stress we may feel in thriving mode is the good stress, *eustress.*

According to psychologist Richard Lazarus, eustress is not defined by what causes a stress but rather how one perceives what is stressing us. Do we see it as a threat or as a challenge? When we choose to see a stressor in a positive way, we are able to respond with a sense of purpose and hope, which contributes to our sense of well-being and satisfaction.

Just like when we are in survival, thriving has a neurological effect on our brain. By focusing on a goal we believe in, our brain produces dopamine, which helps us feel good and broadens our perspective. In thriving mode, all our brain processes are working; we are able to see more options and opportunities because we have access to more data. Our brain is in learning mode and makes new connections and innovations.

You have experienced being in thriving mode and its benefits. You have also experienced being in survival mode and that feeling of being trapped or cornered. The question becomes how to have what mode you are in not be happenstance, determined by circumstance. In the next chapter, we will start to see how you can get your power back, through choice.

CHAPTER 5

The Mindful Game—Choice

You have now been introduced to two ways to approach how you react to things, especially things that you may not prefer. We can be in survival mode or thriving mode. What many of us have lost sight of or forgotten is that we have a choice of which mode we want to be in. The good news is that we will be spending the rest of the book on how you can consciously make that choice.

At any given moment, you are in one mode or the other, thriving or surviving (figure 13).

You cannot be doing both at the same time.

Where do you think most people spend the majority of their time?

Figure 13: Thriving beyond Survival model

If you said survival, you may be right, especially when it comes to the working world. According to Gallup, in 2011 up to 70 percent of workers were disengaged, not thriving, just trying to survive, and protecting themselves. They spent their energy avoiding getting into trouble instead of focusing on their goals or looking for solutions.

During my speaking engagements and workshops, I ask people what side of the model they believe most people live in, and they always point to the survival side. When you think about it, there is a lot of agreement out there that would point to this being the case. Beliefs such as life is a struggle, life isn't fair, and it's a dog-eat-dog world abound. We are constantly being told that we need to be the best and be perfect—but also to fit in and not to rock the boat.

People have bought into the idea that success equals being rich and famous or climbing the corporate ladder; once you are successful, then you will be happy and fulfilled. Or once you marry your soul mate, you will be happy and fulfilled. You need to be macho. You need to be pretty. You should go to college and get a degree. You need to buy, eat, drive, or wear this to be happy and fulfilled. You need to do as you are told. All of these are beliefs that we have inherited and then made our own without much examination.

We have a lot of agreement that survival is the norm; if you look at every newscast and most television shows, it is about people being in survival mode. And there is nothing wrong with being in survival mode, because it has served the function of keeping humans alive on this planet for thousands of years. It is just not where we are most productive or happiest. And our bodies were not meant to spend most of our time there.

How many of these beliefs have we inherited and taken on as the truth—not as our choice but as what has been told to us over and over? And if we believe these things are the ultimate truth, we will find plenty of proof and continue to feel stuck.

If these beliefs were supportive and aligned to goals that we believed were important and meaningful, it would not be a problem. But many of these beliefs are not aligned with our desire to be creative and happy. They distract us from what we really want. Many people give up on their dreams, on the thought that they cannot do the things that fulfill them. People give them up because they believe their goals are just pipe dreams, not reality, and then they see all the proof of that at the exclusion of any other options or opportunities that suggest otherwise.

Now where would you rather spend more of your time? In survival mode or thriving?

You have that choice every moment, even if you don't realize it.

Speaking for myself, I want to spend more of my time in thriving mode.

Mabel, in our story, wants to get back to thriving too. So a mindful game for Mabel and for the rest of us is to find ways to get from survival mode back to thriving and to increase our time in thriving so that we are more productive and having fun along the way.

The danger feels so real, and so survival often seems to be the only or best option available when we are triggered. It becomes the automatic, unthinking response. But in order to increase our time in thriving beyond survival, we need to increase our awareness of the other options and choose the best of them, not settle for the automatic reaction.

Our choice of how we react is the one thing we have complete control over.

We don't really have much control of events that are happening around us, either the situations or the people. I can type on my computer and determine what letters get typed, but I have no control over when the power goes out unexpectedly or the computer crashes.

I really don't have any control over other people. I can believe that I am making someone do what I want, but people are less controllable than electric outages or the weather. Having some influence is the most I can hope for with things that are going on outside of me. All of these points bring me to the plain conclusion that the only thing that I have any real control over is how I react.

How much can we truly know? There are still many things we don't understand about the world around us, much less what is going on inside us and our brains. And we are never really looking at things objectively. Even in scientific experiments, there is what is known as experimenters' bias, which can creep in unconsciously from the prereading they do to the conclusions they draw when interpreting the data. Subjects may even change their behavior from unintentional signals they get from those conducting experiments. And this is considering the intention of the scientist to be as objective as possible.

We choose how we are going to measure things around us through our beliefs.

Our beliefs create our filters, which determine what we focus on. I can change the world around me through the filters that I look through. The data may still be the same, but the meaning will be vastly different. My experience and decisions will be completely different depending on the filter I choose.

The world that changes is only mine; I can change my filter and even toggle back and forth like you can switch between apps on your phone or computer. My world can transform and change while I am sitting still in my chair, and people sitting right next to me will not even notice, because how they see the world is through the filters they believe they are stuck with.

However, we are not stuck with our filters, even though we may believe we are. Reality is not as concrete as we fear. We like certainty and tend to solidify the reality around us because it lets us have a cohesive storyline, one that we can manipulate to make sense of and predict what will happen tomorrow. This is all good. It allows us to plan and to not have to focus on everything (those eleven million data points) so that we become overwhelmed.

The fact is that everything is not certain, and that is actually good news. It means that new things are possible.

Playing a mindful game will have you experience the different worlds that you can live in. The more we are aware and consciously change our filters, the more we can see that we have control of our experiences and that transformation is possible.

Remember—when our story changes, so do we.

A few years ago, I experienced a day that was going great, and I was feeling how good life was. I loved my job. My role was supporting executives in creating their development plans and discussing the development needs of their direct reports. I also had special requests from leaders to facilitate their team-building sessions. My boss was supportive of me and acknowledged the difference I was making. I had coworkers that I liked and who liked me. I was happy.

When I got home that evening, I received a call from a friend who was canceling on our plans—again. I felt like she really didn't want to get together. I had thoughts of being brushed off, not being appreciated. Then I got a call from my mom complaining about her money situation. She never asked me how I was or what was going on in my life. I was feeling invisible.

Nothing had changed at work from the day before, but I remember waking up and dreading going to the office. I got an e-mail from my boss with a request, and it felt like he was imposing on me and giving me meaningless things to do and that he was not valuing me. As I walked into the office, all my coworkers seemed to be either ignoring me or complaining about their own issues. I felt an emotion of sadness and hopelessness. Life did not seem good.

I remember thinking to myself how starkly different these two days were. I left work the day before in one world and was entering the office in a completely different one. Nothing at work had changed; the situation was the same. Why did it feel so dreadful today? Why was it now a place I didn't want to be? Now, mind you, I had come up with a list of reasons why things were so dreary and what was making me feel this way: coworkers' behavior, my boss, the tone of the e-mail, and more. And before becoming mindful and understanding the model, I would have bought into the story my brain was making up and muscled through the day, hoping that something good would happen so that I could feel better.

But this time, I really looked at the data. I became conscious that what was going on at work today was not different from yesterday. The situation was identical. I had the same role, same coworkers, and same boss. What had changed was how I was viewing things. The evening before had triggered an unconscious belief and a fear of being unvalued and invisible. That filter was still in place when I woke up, and my brain was finding proof everywhere, interpreting what was happening in order to fit the story. I was fascinated at how different my experience was of the same situation. It was that day that I truly saw that it was my filter that had changed, not the world. And if it was my filter, I was the one in control.

It's a Matter of Choice—Really

Now is your chance to realize you can change your filter; you can opt into the side you want to be on—thriving or surviving.

And maybe you really like the drama. If you do, then choose it. Be aware of what your game is and what result you are really going for. You can find enjoyment in that experience if you are choosing it consciously.

Most people who are in survival are there by default; they are unwittingly putting themselves in the position of victim. If you are right that things are wrong, and it is your enemy's fault, then you are at the mercy of your enemy, a perpetual victim.

I think that is a part of why many of us are so trapped in survival, even when we understand that it is a matter of focusing on the positive. In those moments, we tend to think that the positives in life are not as real or valid as the problems we are facing. There is a belief that if you are not worried or anxious about things that are not going your way, you are not facing reality. Somehow negative things are more valid. Could this have originated from the child who was always taught that being a grown-up is a serious business, and it's better to prepare for the worst? So even if we think we want to stop worrying, we are afraid to because we think that the worry is some type of protection, a way to prevent what we are afraid of from happening. Understanding how our filters work, we can now see that the opposite is true. We end up being more aware of what we don't want and become blind to opportunities that come our way.

But if you are aware of your power to choose and consciously choose to be in the drama at any given moment, that makes you more powerful than being in survival mode by default.

If you know you are choosing to stay in the drama, you know you have the choice to get out. You have probably heard people say "but I have no choice" when they are caught in survival mode. And this is where a lot of the feeling of being trapped comes from. You feel you have no choice because the only options you are seeing are fight-or-flight options, and deep down, we know that is a no-win situation. But the reality is that it is never a no-choice situation.

I remember having breakfast with a friend who was smack-dab in the middle of survival mode. She was a mother of two and a business owner who did a lot of work from home. Her husband worked at the house too. She believed that she never had any alone time and that her time was totally monopolized by her family and business. She felt trapped, and the only two choices she saw that she had were to either abandon her family or suffer. Neither option was one that she wanted, but no matter what I said, she argued that she "had no other choice." She couldn't see the irony that she was spending an hour and a half in a restaurant with me, who was not her family or business, fighting to prove that she had no control of her time.

So if you consciously choose to spend time in survival mode (because sometimes you just need to vent, let out the negative energy), you consciously know you can choose to thrive. You are not trapped. There is an option available that will have better outcomes and create more opportunities to have what you really want, something more than just being right.

Playing a Mindful Game

Most of us want to increase our time in thriving.

The mindful game then is to know when you are in thriving mode and appreciate the journey—and know when you are in survival mode and look for ways to get back to thriving. The mindful game is choosing which side of the model *you* want to spend most of your time in: thriving or surviving.

What is important to remember is that the game is not about never being in survival mode or avoiding survival mode at all costs. That is impossible to achieve, and if you set it as a goal (perfection), it will keep you trapped. The more you try to avoid and ignore survival mode, the more you fall into it. Survival mode is part of the human experience. It provides good information and helps to alert you to danger or to a belief that is not aligned with your goals. Though it can feel very uncomfortable, there is nothing wrong with being in survival mode. It is just not where you are meant to spend most of your life.

The object of the mindful game is to increase the time we spend in thriving mode.

Since the majority of us feel trapped when in survival mode, part two of this book will give you several strategies you can use to get back to thriving mode. Then we will look at ways to stay in thriving mode longer.

PART 2

Your Thriving Playbook

CHAPTER 6

Game Play

Now that you know the layout of your choices and are ready to play a mindful game, it is beneficial to know some strategies that you can use to support you in not only succeeding but increasing your skill and continuously leveling up.

In this next part of the book, we will go over five strategies that work for me in staying in my mindful game of thriving and participating with others who may or may not be in the same game. Though there are some directions for how you can get from survival mode back to thriving, these are not steps that need to be taken in order or specific to-dos. They are strategies to support you in not only seeing the choices you have but actually making the choices that move you into life as you prefer it.

When you apply any of these strategies, you will start to see noticeable changes in your results. You will find yourself reacting, feeling, and seeing things differently, which will change your perception of the situation. You will notice outcomes that are more in line with what you prefer. How quickly or gradually you experience these shifts will depend on the level of survival that you are in. The more you practice these strategies and the more you notice the positive changes, the more preferable outcomes you will get. It becomes a positive cycle.

Strategy 1: Awareness

What are you focused on? Are you focused on what is happening now, what's in the future, or what happened in the past?

Developing your awareness of the present is a key to keeping you in the game of thriving. Your goal is to become mindful of what you are feeling and thinking in any situation.

The idea is not to eliminate negative emotions. That is not possible. The game is about using our emotions as the guide they are and not the trap we have let them become.

Your emotions are an effective indicator of being in thriving or survival mode. If you are feeling focused, happy, and engaged, you are thriving and can easily create a sense of appreciation for what you are experiencing.

If you are feeling a negative emotion such as frustration, anger, or fear, your filter has detected something that you have programmed as a danger. You are being alerted, and if you are aware of this, you have a choice of whether to fall into survival mode or stay on track with your goals.

When you are triggered with a negative emotion, it is not about the situation that is happening now but about how this situation is similar to ones you have had in the past that felt dangerous. You think you recognize your tiger, and you react with fight or flight.

By paying attention to how you are feeling, checking in with your emotions, you are able to be more mindful to what is really going on (is this really a tiger? Perhaps it's an opportunity to improve a relationship) and better able to catch yourself before you go into your automatic survival response. It isn't about denying your emotions or making yourself feel something you don't; it is about paying attention to your feelings so that you, not your emotions, can be in control. If you are able to stop and be aware, you may give your higher brain processes time to stay in the picture. Then you will have the opportunity to choose what you want to focus on, how you would prefer to feel, and the most beneficial actions you can take.

Mabel has been in survival mode for a few weeks; she can't sleep and is noticing that most of her conversations, even at home, are about her situation at work. She realizes that she is in survival mode and misses the happy, productive worker she used to be.

She takes a moment to really notice how she is feeling and writes the emotions down. On her list, she has embarrassed, worried, and fearful as her main negative emotions. She becomes very conscious of the complaints she has been broadcasting to her friends and family. Her biggest complaint is that her boss doesn't value her or the contribution she makes.

She thinks back on her first meeting with him and how her supervisor reacted to the situation. Mabel realizes that she has been very tentative and cautious about her work ever since that first day. Before the incident, her main focus was on the department goals and doing top-notch work. Lately, she has not thought about how the department as a whole has been doing because she has been feeling paranoid about her own performance.

She can see how trapped she has become, and in uncovering this, she can now choose to climb out of survival mode.

Choosing what to focus on and how to feel is not always easy, especially when you are just starting to play your mindful game of thriving. It is much easier to just give into your automatic reaction. One reason is because this belief (that situations like this are a danger) is an unconscious habit, and so it feels true without having to examine it. Another reason is that the survival response to danger is instinctual. There is some hardwiring involved.

The task is not to alter your alert system that warns you of danger; there is value in having an unconscious part of you working to keep you alive. What awareness brings is the ability to distinguish everyday survival mode from true life-and-death situations. With this distinction, you can respond appropriately.

What do I mean about checking in with your emotions?

This is similar to our earlier discussion of mindfulness.

👉 Create a practice of consciously asking yourself how you are feeling at moments throughout your day—not to be self-conscious, to be mindful. When you are not feeling good emotionally, name the emotion and identify how it is feeling in your body. This will put you in the present moment and allow you to become more aware of what triggered the emotion and what your beliefs and fears about the situation may be.

Now, here's a tip that will make this practice much more effective for you. Practice doing this when you are feeling good. If you practice at those times when you are *not* triggered with a negative emotion, it will be easier to check in when you do get frustrated or overwhelmed.

Understanding Your Alarm

When in survival mode, what triggered you about this situation is its similarity to a danger you experienced in the past, so your automatic response will be to fit the facts to that past story, which may not be appropriate to the situation now. When you are aware of this tendency and know you are feeling a negative emotion, you can now be aware that what has been triggered is a *belief* and may not be the truth. This is good news! Remember—we can change a belief. If it is the truth, we are stuck.

When you increase your awareness of your emotions and catch yourself being triggered before you react, it gives you a chance to alert yourself to be more observant, to slow down the impulses of fight or flight. You will have time to take a deep breath and know that even if you can't see all of them clearly right now, you have more options than you think.

You have the opportunity to also become very aware of what is happening in the present moment, so that you can identify what set off the warning signal and take appropriate action. It's like your smoke detector.

When your smoke detector goes off, it is a signal that there may be a danger, so you take appropriate action, all the while looking for what caused the danger. As quickly as possible, you engage your brain and your muscles to move if necessary. If it is in the middle of the night, and you see or smell smoke, you get yourself and your loved ones out of the house. However, if it is in the middle of the day, and there is no smoke or burning smell, or if it was because you were frying some chicken and forgot to turn on the vent, you take action that is appropriate to that situation. You don't run out of the house because the alarm went off. And you don't ignore the alarm. The alarm has done its job to help you take the best action quickly. And you *appreciate* that the alarm works.

Negative emotions are like your smoke detector. Having negative emotions does not mean that what you feel is invalid or that you have the whole situation wrong and you should just force yourself to be happy about it. The fact may be that something is happening that is an obstacle in the path of your goal. It may be someone not agreeing or saying no, someone steering things in another direction or another unforeseen obstacle. If you are aware of feeling frustrated, you now have a choice of how you will fit the situation into your story. You can choose if you will use the situation as proof that you have enemies and that they are out to keep you from what you want. Or you can refocus on your goal, look at the new information, and take appropriate action that moves you forward.

It's Your Choice

I am constantly checking in with how I am feeling emotionally. I find this practice very beneficial. I remember a time when I was a manager in my department and my director would call and give me menial, administrative things to do that were not part of my duties. It would make me feel very indignant. Didn't he know that this was not part of my role and I had more productive things to do with my time? Doing the tasks became such a chore that I would fume and complain to my coworkers every time he made that type of request.

I remember becoming aware of feeling this way when I received yet another e-mail with one of these tasks. This time though, I stopped and took a moment to become aware of the emotion that I was feeling, and I saw that I was frustrated and indignant because I thought that he was not valuing me or my time. I was poised to fight the good fight of deserving respect. This was actually not about what was happening now but about a past-based fear. When I really listened to my feelings, knowing that this was a belief, not the truth, I saw that this situation triggered my fear that I *was not* valuable, and I was using his requests to perform small clerical tasks as proof that I was right! That became an ah-ha moment because I wouldn't have thought that I had that fear. Once I uncovered the belief, I had the opportunity to choose a new belief, the belief that I do make a difference.

By paying attention to how we are feeling, we are able to be more mindful of what is really going on and catch ourselves before we go into our automatic survival response. Remember it isn't about not feeling our emotions or making ourselves feel something we don't; it is more about paying attention to our feelings so that we can be in control and not go into our automatic response. If we are able to stop and be aware, we may give our higher brain processes time to stay in the picture. And not surprisingly, we gain more positive outcomes.

Awareness Is the First Step in Changing a Habit

It is not about the situation; it is about how you are *feeling* about the situation that is at issue, because how you feel is an indication of what you believe the situation is about. Remember your actions will follow your beliefs.

So in addition to being aware of your feelings, also listen to the story and/or complaints you are telling others and saying to yourself.

What is it that you need to prove or are afraid of? Just like listening to the feedback from others, listen to your own. If this feedback is not valid, you can discard it. You do not have to believe everything you think.

Being in thriving mode means that you are able to stay focused on what you really want to accomplish. It means you feel respect and appreciation for the situation and people involved, and it means you will take action that will be in line with progressing toward your goal. It may be that previous actions and their driving beliefs need to be adjusted. You are learning.

How to Change a Belief

As I stated before, beliefs can be tricky because they are often unconscious habits, and so they don't seem to be beliefs but occur as the "truth." Once we have accepted an old belief that is no longer useful, we think we have no options or ability to change what is happening. But when we step back and question what we believe is true, we can uncover how it is our beliefs are shaping how we perceive things, which gives us the power to change our beliefs.

Here is a simple exercise that you can take yourself through. Try this when you are feeling safe and not deep in survival mode.

Think about a situation and the outcome or goal that you prefer for that situation. Write down what your beliefs are around the goals you have. What do you believe makes this goal worth pursuing? What do you believe will make it possible? Are there obstacles that you believe are too big to overcome? Do you have lists of reasons why it can never happen to you?

Listing your beliefs and noting which ones are positive and which ones are negative will allow you to see which ones you are focused on proving true, the ones that keep you moving toward your goal or the ones that are distracting you from what you say you want.

You may look at your list of beliefs and have the feeling that one is a truth, not a belief. Let's take a common one:

"I have no time to do what needs to be done to accomplish this."

Consider that in order to know this is actually true, a fact, you would need to be able to predict the future 100 percent. Can you? If you are like most of us, you can't, so the statement that you will have no time is not the truth. It is a belief, and you are more focused on proving it true than you are on accomplishing what you say you want. So you have a choice of relooking at your goal and determining if it really is something that you prefer, and if it is, to refocus on accomplishing the goal rather than proving that the belief that you have no time is true. This will allow you to see options that you may not have seen before because you stopped looking for options the moment you said that you had no time.

Your Emotions

Doing the above exercise works best with those beliefs that you are conscious about. However, there are many beliefs that we have that are so much of a habit that we are not conscious of what it is we believe that is stopping us.

Your unconscious beliefs reveal themselves through your emotions. It is sometimes difficult to be able to state what those beliefs may be. That's okay. You feel the emotion first, and then your mind fits the situation to your belief. So a way to change the habit of unconscious beliefs is by working on giving yourself different emotions to choose from.

☞ Make a list of the specific emotions that you feel when you think about a specific situation that is important to you, but you can't overcome feeling stuck.

Put the positive emotions on the thriving side and the negative emotions on the survival side of the list. Leave a space across from each word. Try to be specific about the emotions that you are feeling. Avoid describing details about the situation. For example, a list of emotions would be "frustrated," "anxious," or "mad," not "he didn't do what I asked" or "the check bounced."

For each negative emotion, think of an opposite positive emotion that you would rather experience, if you had the choice.

Table 1
Example

Thriving	Surviving
Competent	
Calm, curious	Frustrated
Appreciation, confidence	Unvalued

For each positive emotion that you wrote down, think of a time when you felt those specific emotions and write a short description of this situation next to that emotion on your list. For example, I felt calm when I took a walk on the beach last week, or I felt confident when I made that presentation to the committee last month. Recall how effective and productive you were when you were feeling positive. As best you can, feel the emotion of the positive situation.

You are now consciously aware that you know how to feel both the positive and the negative emotions.

Your brain had associated the negative emotion with any situation that seemed similar to an original situation that you determined was a danger, and that negative emotion had become the automatic choice.

There is nothing wrong with the negative emotion. It's just that your actions associated with the emotion will usually be going into fight/flight, looking for agreement, and accumulating proof/evidence to prove that you are right. These are not actions that move you toward your goal.

Up until now, feeling those negative emotions has not really been a choice; it's been your default that you put in place to protect you.

Now, take a look at each set of emotions, reminding yourself that you know how to feel both the positive emotions that you prefer and the negative emotions that have been a habit. Realize that you have the ability to choose, in this moment, which emotion you want to feel from now on in this type of situation.

Making this conscious choice sends information to the unconscious part of your brain that regulates emotion. Now, circle the emotion you want to choose going forward.

Pay attention to how you are feeling and remind yourself that you have a choice.

Having a choice isn't about forcing yourself to feel something that you don't feel in the moment. It is about becoming conscious that you do ultimately have a choice in your emotions.

Here are some things to practice when building your skills in the area of awareness.

New Mindful Game Play: Awareness

Questions to ask yourself:

- How am I feeling right now?
- What am I thinking (over and over)?
- What am I saying (over and over)?

Actions to take:

- List beliefs both positive and negative and choose which to put your focus and attention on (see "How to Change a Belief" section.)
- List negative emotions you may be feeling and then the positive emotions you prefer. Remember when you experienced those positive emotions and that you know how to feel both sets of emotions. Then consciously choose which ones you want to feel going forward (see "Your Emotions" section.)

Strategy 2: The Object of Your Game—Your Goals

As we discussed earlier, in order to play any game, you need to know the object of the game—the goal.

In a mindful game of thriving, your goal is your picture of the outcome or the result that you prefer. With this goal, you have a means of measuring progress and an ability to adjust to stay on course, along with knowing when you have succeeded. At the beginning of this book, you were instructed to create such a goal.

This goal and others you create will be central in keeping you in a mindful game of thriving.

If we have no preferred result that we have thought about or articulated, the default goal is to survive, and we find ourselves in a long game of drama. Having a goal allows you to have a focal point that is another option than just surviving.

Furthermore, creating a goal that is more meaningful to you than being right becomes the beacon that will guide you back to thriving in those times when you find yourself in survival mode.

If you weren't able to come up with a goal or you are not sure what it is that you want, here are some suggestions.

- **Pay attention to things that catch your interest throughout your day.** This will help you to determine the things that you like, that excite you, and that would put you on a course that will be meaningful for you.

- **Make lists of what you like and want to do, have, or experience in your life.** You can start with a list of what you know you *don't* want and then use it to make the list of what you do want. Your goals can be general things you would like such as make a difference, be happy, be an effective leader—you get to determine what success will be for you. Your goals can also be specific, such as learn to play the guitar, take a trip to India, or increase sales.

- **Gauge how you feel when you picture yourself with whatever it is you want.** If you are feeling excited and happy, you are on the right track. Keep going. If you are feeling anxious, your focus may be back on what you don't want—your fear that you can't have what you want or that you don't know how to get it. This is a habit. Remind yourself that at this point, you are only making a list of what you want; you don't need to know the how. Take a break and come back to your list at a later time.

Review your list and mark out anything that is there because you feel like it *should* be on your list or because someone else put it there. This list is about what *you want,* not what you have been told you should want.

As we talked about earlier, if you are in a role that has certain goals and responsibilities that you *need* to accomplish, even though you may not have chosen them, take a moment to think about the big picture. See what a bigger goal may be for you that you can choose to opt into and include those responsibilities as part of your mindful game of thriving.

Some Things to Keep in Mind about the Goals That You Create

When you have come up with a list of things that you want to have, do, or experience in your life, you can create goals around each of those preferred items. Here are some things to keep in mind to experience your goals as fun.

- **Goals are about results or outcomes that you want to have, not your to-do list.** Remember that goals inform your actions. If there comes a time when you are not making progress, don't give up on your goal; instead, adjust your actions.
- **Goals are not an end game; the point is not just to accomplish the goal but to have fun along the way.** The best goals are those that will enable you to enjoy the anticipation, the planning of details, and the overall journey. Once you have accomplished one goal, there will always be the "Now what?" opportunity to plan what's next.
- **Don't get bogged down or too attached to what the end result may look like.** Before I made my trip to India, I had an idea of what it would be like from pictures and stories that I heard. The actual experience was nothing that I could have imagined even with the information I had. If I had been attached to what I thought the experience should have been, I would have been blind to the amazing reality it turned out to be. Many times, the goal we want is something new for us, and we only have a limited view of what success might look like. Have your vision clear enough to stay on course but not so concrete that you will miss a result that is better than you could ever imagine.

How Do You Use Your Goals to Get Back to Thriving?

Think of your goals as a lighthouse beacon to keep you on track when you notice that you are in survival mode.

Remember my example with the boss giving me the perceived menial tasks that would frustrate me? When I realized I was in survival mode because I was itching to go complain to a coworker and get agreement, I knew I wanted to get back to thriving mode. After identifying my emotions, I reminded myself of my goal of being a valuable employee and making a difference for the people I work with. When I refocused on this, I could see that, for my boss, it wasn't about valuing an employee or not; for him it was about finding a way to get something done that he couldn't or didn't know how to do.

Now I understand that when we are in the throes of survival, we are not always thinking clearly, and if we haven't thought of our goals recently, they are hard to remember.

A practice that I do and recommend is keeping a journal especially for your goals. I write my goals at a regular time every day. This habit has not only made it easier to remember what is most important to me, it has created a habit for me of focusing on what I want and looking for opportunities and options to get the results I prefer. As a result, time I spend focusing on what I don't want or what may not be going the way I would like has been greatly reduced.

This practice will also remind you to be aware of all the results that you have accomplished, not just the fact that you crossed something off a to-do list.

Mabel chooses to get back in touch with the goals that she prefers and her beliefs that are aligned with those goals. She puts her focus on the contribution she makes to the whole department with her expertise and productivity and how that benefits the customers she works with, instead of her fear of being seen as a slacker. She knows she wants to make a difference for her customers and coworkers with her collaborative spirit. And she creates a new goal of developing a good and respectful relationship with her supervisor.

Here are some practices that will help you get better at the strategy of using your goals as a point of focus.

New Mindful Game Play: Goals

Questions to ask yourself:

- What are my goals?
- What are goals I have taken on that are not mine?
- What do I prefer for this situation?
- What would be a win/win?
- What do I want to experience next?
- What are things that will engage me?

Actions to practice:

- Keep a goal journal for your short- and long-term preferred outcomes.
- Use your goal to focus on like a lighthouse beacon.
- Create goals you can opt into around current responsibilities.

Distinguishing Success and Failure

An advantage of opting in and playing a mindful game of thriving is that you are able to consciously define what success and failure are for you. We all want to be successful and not fail. The question is what are we defining as success, and what do we believe is the danger of failure?

I remember reading an article on the top ten things the most successful people do. Reading the list made me exhausted. I wasn't sure what the value of success was from the article because it was all about working harder and longer than everyone else. That is a no-win situation because there will always be someone who works harder or longer, and so you can never rest. How was all this success *benefiting* these most successful people? Were they really enjoying themselves?

Society, parents, teachers, and experts attempt to define what success is for others, but it is really only something that can be defined by the individual, by you. Trying to live up to someone else's definition of success almost always puts us into survival mode. We have our own goals and dreams, and we are the only ones who can determine success for ourselves.

But many of us have not really examined what our beliefs are around success and failure. Many times, it is not the anticipation of success that drives us but the fear of failure.

Becoming aware of what your current beliefs of success and failure are and consciously choosing beliefs about both will give you a huge boost in staying in your game of thriving.

When in survival mode, success is commonly defined as:

- **something determined by others**
  Growing up, we were told when we were being good or bad by our parents, given a grade by our teachers, and rated on our performance by our boss, all in things that they wanted us to achieve or what was set as *the* standard. We have been trained to view success by what others have determined as the measure. These beliefs of success may not be what we really want.

- **a moment in time**

  "I will be successful when I win the championship" is an example of success being a moment in time. If this is our dominant definition, what happens when the game is over?

- **money/fame/position**

  When we buy into the belief that success is the traditional money/fame/position, we are usually expecting to finally feel happy, confident, or worthy once we have acquired the dollar amount, the VP position, or see our name in lights. What many have found is that they feel the same way when they reached the goal as they did on the way. So if they were not feeling happy or confident or worthy while acquiring the money/fame/position, they don't feel it when they get there, so they either crash or try to climb higher. There is nothing wrong with wanting money/fame/position if it is what we really want and see it as a blast getting there; it is when we believe it is something that we should want or have because of what society or others have told us we should want that puts us in survival mode.

- **proof we are good enough**

  "I'll show them" has been a driver for many people reaching goals that they have set and relentlessly worked toward no matter what the consequences were to their health, relationships, or happiness. This is another no-win, never-ending scenario because if we are proving to someone (and ourselves) that we are good enough, it is because there is a belief that we are not, and no matter what gets accomplished, our filters will always be on the lookout and showing us evidence that we are not good enough. We are never able to fully appreciate any success we accomplish.

- **result of working harder and struggling more than everyone else**

  With this belief, success is about working hard and struggling. So you will always be working hard and struggling. Not much room for thriving. Also, there is always the possibility that someone is working harder than you, and looking out for this will consume your time and the satisfaction you would have had reaching a goal.

Do any of these sound familiar? When you think about the definitions and beliefs that you have, you may come up with others that you would add to this list. Think about how you feel about success, and if there is any resistance or a feeling of "showing them" or proving yourself, consider that the definitions are from the survival side, and you may want to create new definitions and beliefs for yourself.

When in thriving mode, beliefs and definitions of success are:

- **determined by you**
  We thrive when we are going toward what we truly want. Even when we are given goals with success criteria, we have the ability to opt in and create how the given goal fits in with our bigger game.
- **progress**
  When we define success as seeing progress toward our goal and not just the achievement of it, we are able to feel a sense of accomplishment along the way, and when we do meet that anticipated result, we are ready for what is next.
- **accomplishments/mastery as an indicator**
  When we see accomplishments as an indicator of progress and not as the ultimate end game, we are able to be excited about what is next and our future growth. A true master is never finished growing and learning. That person is not concerned with being designated as "the best," because they are excited about what new levels they can reach.

Any awards or achievements are just indicators of their progress.

- **continuously growing and expanding**
- **being happy and engaged**

Most of us have a mixture of the two sets of definitions because there are things that we have felt very successful with, that have brought us that feeling of being in the flow and thriving—but the other definitions we have keep pulling us into survival and may have us feel like we are driving with the emergency brake on. We may move forward, but it is with a lot of effort and always uphill.

Playing a mindful game of thriving means choosing your goal and determining what success is for you. Uncovering what beliefs you have that do not benefit you allows you to choose what you want to believe about success for yourself going forward. Thinking about your definition and emotions and connecting those with your now consciously chosen beliefs about success will let you know if you are succeeding.

An important part of freeing yourself from the seemingly continuous uphill battle that we have associated with success is to become aware of the beliefs you have around failure. Like I stated before, our fear of failure may be more of a driver than our desire for success.

See if you may have some of the following beliefs around failure lurking in your unconscious.

When in survival mode, failure is commonly defined as:

- **determined by others**
  Just as we have been trained to look to others as to when we have succeeded, we have also bought into the belief that it is others who determine if we fail. This has us doing things that we don't want to do. How many of you believe that you

are a failure in some way if you are a certain age and not yet married, making a certain income, owning a house ...

- **dangerous**
- **proof of inability/unworthiness/incompetence**
- **losing**
- **labels/defines you**
- **judgment**
- **deserves to be punished**

Just as we have defined success as an event, we often define losing as a judgment or label. If we fail, then we have a belief, maybe unconscious, that we are a failure, and then our filter is set to that belief. When we feel the fear of failure coming on, our filter will show us all the reasons we failed in the past and will fail in the future, and because we are in survival mode, we look for an enemy to blame. It's a trap that distracts us from taking action toward what we really want.

To redefine failure in a way that lets us use it as a tool to help us grow and learn starts with believing that failure is totally in our power to redefine. There is a lot of agreement that failure is a danger and that if you make one false move, it will ruin the rest of your life. On the other hand, there are many examples of people who have failed big, and their lives turned out just fine. President Lincoln lost in elections five times before he was elected president. He didn't define failure as proof that he was unworthy. Inspirational stories abound about people who did not let failure define them; they redefined failure.

Here are some new definitions of failure that you can use going forward.

When in thriving mode, beliefs and definitions of failure are:

- **chance to learn**
- **indicator of veering off track**
- **new information to make adjustments (feedback)**
- **a way to increase the quickness of mastery**
- **indicator of growth**

We have all made mistakes and learned from them, so you have some beliefs around failure that have kept you in survival. Take some time to consciously define what failure is to you and associate it with those feelings you have had of learning and growing.

Strategy 3: Playing the Game—Actions

Let's check in with Mabel.

Now that Mabel has refocused on what she really wants, she considers her next action that will move her toward her goals of having a good relationship with her supervisor and being a valuable contributor to her team and customers. She acknowledges that complaining is not one of those actions and is resolved to stop talking about how bad she sees her situation.

She makes a list of things that she can do, including bringing up her production number, agreeing to take on a project she was about to pass up because she was worried about failing, and most importantly, talking to her supervisor to get more facts. What are his expectations and feedback? How does he really feel about her performance? She wants to find out how she can better contribute to the goals he has for the department. She realizes that she had not really paid attention to what his vision for the department was because she was so focused on finding proof that he was wrong.

Taking actions that are consistent with your goals and not the activities of survival (fight or flight, getting agreement, gathering proof and evidence) is a big step in getting back to thriving mode.

When Mabel takes the new actions she comes up with, no matter how she may feel in the moment, she is letting her unconscious brain know that this situation is not a danger and to focus on her main goals. The situation will not feel as dangerous, and she will gain a sense of balance.

If you are aware of your emotions, and you have refocused on what you really want, you can then be conscious of the next action you are about to take. You again have a choice, and no matter what you choose, there is power in the choosing. It is no longer just automatic.

So what are your choices? You can go into fight or flight, do nothing, or take deliberate actions toward a goal that you have created and prefer.

Action Choices

When I caught myself getting frustrated with my boss's request and having the ah-ha of my fear, I was able to refocus on my true goal of being a valuable employee. I was still feeling the emotions of frustration but consciously decided that the action I was going to take was to do the task requested, though this time it was not because I had to but because it was an action that was moving me toward my goal of adding value to those I work with. I was in essence informing my unconscious brain that this type of situation was no longer a danger, and it did not need to filter for it anymore.

Guess what happened the next time my boss gave me another one of these tasks? It did not bother me as much. I may have been mildly annoyed, but that was easy to let go of. And it got to the point where I did not have an emotional reaction at all. I no longer had to use situations like this to prove that I might not be adding value.

Something to Keep in Mind

I have to admit that during this situation when I was in survival and before I applied the model, I was holding on to another belief that I think is common to many of us and keeps us trapped. When we are in survival mode, part of what keeps perpetuating our being stuck is the belief that if we don't make someone wrong, if we don't stop them and punish them, it will mean that we are letting them get away with something, and they will just keep doing it, not only to us but to others. This thought gave me more justification for finding proof of how wrong my boss was. The problem with this line of thinking is that my perception of what he was doing had to do with my beliefs about myself and was not an accurate reflection of his motives. It blinded me from the bigger picture and what my part was in creating my experience. It distracted me from my choice of taking action toward my goal.

But what about when people do horrible things like open fire at a school? Shouldn't they be punished? Aren't we more justified in seeking retribution? We can't just let people like that get away with it, can we? This line of thinking still gets us distracted from what we really want. Anger and the need to have to punish someone is what caused the situation; anger will not be what prevents it. What is at the root cause of these incidents, as Scarlett Lewis stated, is when someone doesn't know they have a choice between love and anger. Our choosing love in our day-to-day life lets others see there are options, and love will always produce better results.

It's Never Too Late to Choose to Thrive

Sometimes you don't become aware that you are in survival mode until after you have taken a fight-or-flight action or are in the middle of a conversation where you are soliciting agreement on how bad the enemy is. The moment you become aware that you are in survival mode, the choice presents itself. You can continue, or you can refocus on your goals, change the conversation, and enter into new dialogue with your opponent rather than plotting against your enemy. Or you can stay in fight or flight until you are tired of it, understanding the result you get from a fight is *just* confirming your belief that you are right. And perhaps your underlying belief is that you are right about being less than worthy. Not much satisfaction in that victory.

Take my friend Glenda's experience, for example.

Breaking in a new boss takes work. This was Glenda's third boss in three years, and she expected he would be her toughest. The two previous directors were hired from inside the company. She knew them before they started managing. She had a sense of who they were and their work styles. It gave her a foundation to quickly build relationships. That was the most important thing for Glenda, the relationship. This new boss was from the outside and was a total unknown; she was going to have to start from scratch.

She thought back to the first meeting with her new executive director, James. He was ex-military, and she sensed that he was both physically and mentally built by the army. His hair was cut short, he had a fit body, and he did not favor chitchat. When she started off the conversation by asking him about his move to a new city and how his family was adjusting, he answered politely but did not ask anything about her family in return. He never asked any questions that let her know he was even interested in her as a person. This had become red flag number one for Glenda.

Glenda was familiar with the distinctions of thriving versus surviving. She had worked her way out of a surviving situation a couple of bosses ago that had her thriving and flowing even through the transition of the director prior to James. She knew the signs, and she sensed that she was in the tornado, as she likes to call survival mode.

It began to build when changes happened that were not making sense to her. She was being given more responsibility on top of the area she was already accountable for. She didn't feel like she was being listened to and was frustrated. Before she was actually aware of what she was doing, she started to show the classic signs of survival mode. She would withdraw in meetings, complain to coworkers, and amass evidence that James was not on her side and was making things difficult for her. She even had members of her team coming to her with data that fueled her complaints.

She was working on her resume and calculating how long she could stay afloat if she were to quit. And she wanted to quit. This is what nibbled at her awareness, to poke through her feeling of fighting the good fight and enable her to acknowledge that she was in survival mode.

"I started picturing the model in my head and knew what side I was on, and though I was in the throes and feeling stuck, my brain was contemplating the steps for getting out," Glenda later told me over lunch. "I knew I was in survival, and I had to figure out what I really wanted, but I had built up so much agreement and evidence, I was beginning to see danger everywhere, and it was hard to switch my focus. But thank goodness I did."

It happened in a one-on-one meeting with her director. He was giving feedback he had received on Glenda's behavior with another leader in the organization. This was so upsetting to Glenda because it was from someone who she had trusted. In that moment, she did something that she would never have thought herself capable of. In front of James, she wrote down the name of the person who had spoken to him on a Post-It note, tore it off the tab, showed it to him, and then proceeded to tear it up. It was at that moment that she saw how deeply she had fallen into the swirl of the vicious cycle that survival mode can put you in. She went into observer mode, which gave her the ability to know she had a choice.

"Thank goodness I had the model, or I would be in a heap of trouble. It was at that moment when I saw that I had a choice to keep swirling and being miserable or to start stating what I wanted and asking questions that would give me the facts and data in a situation where I was making a lot of negative assumptions. And the moment I saw I had a choice, it got quiet in my head. It was like I got dropped out of the tornado, and I started to stand up for me and what was important for me. I was able to have a real conversation with James, let him know what was working and not working, what I needed and what I needed to know. He gave me information that at first was hard to take, but I was able to look at it as feedback and decide if I was willing to opt in. I saw that I was up for the challenge, and my whole world changed. I was out of survival and back in thriving."

What was important about this experience for Glenda was that in the moment she became fully conscious and aware that she was in survival mode, she saw she had a choice of either continuing or choosing to get back to thriving. Even though she was in a tense situation, she chose thriving and was able to refocus in real time on what she really wanted. She then saw more options for her next actions, which altered the outcome of the situation for the better.

There may be times when you become aware of your anger, hurt, or frustration at its height, and it takes every ounce of will to not do or say anything, knowing that it will be counterproductive. And the most you find you can do is recite "they are not the enemy" in your head.

For many of you, doing nothing is noticeably different behavior. And you may find that people are surprised, try harder to get the reaction that they are used to getting from you, or give you agreement on how right you are and wrong the enemy is without you even asking or looking for it. This is when you know that you are making progress.

You may also start to hear the beliefs that you have unconsciously made into truth in your head. Things like, "This always happens to me," "They don't value me; see, I can't make a difference," "I don't know what I am doing, and they are going to find out I'm a fraud," or "Everyone is against me." These are phrases I have heard in my own head. And there is an inference our brain makes that this situation is proof of that belief and that is what we are really fighting against. That belief is what is making the situation feel dangerous, not what may be happening. In fact, what seems a danger for you may not be what others in the situation are even thinking or intending.

Improvement Comes with Practice

The more I am in thriving, the more I see that most people want to support and contribute to others. It is just hard to do when you are constantly in survival mode.

Once you begin to take actions toward what you want instead of reacting to the belief that there is a danger, even if it is nonaction, you are consciously reprogramming that part of your brain that is looking for danger. You are letting it know that this type of situation is no longer a threat and can be taken off the watch list. What will happen is that you notice the alarm sooner, and your reaction alters. It may be where you hear the phrases in your head, like "You never catch a break, you should be upset about this," and your emotions are feeling balanced. Or you feel a negative emotion, but you don't hear any chatter in your head that states that you need to prove that you are right.

In both of these scenarios, you are able to focus quickly and fully on your goal and the next best action to take. Your brain is realizing that it has a choice, and it is opting for the choice that feels better and gets better results. It is diffusing the alarm system tied to equating this situation with danger.

You are not only becoming more effective in the moment, you are also making it easier to deal with similar situations in the future, and there will come a time when you will say to yourself, "A few months ago, that would have sent me off the deep end, but now it is not even an issue for me and is easy to deal with."

And if there is a real life-or-death danger, you will find that you are able to see more options for being safe, you panic less, and you are ready to take more focused and effective action.

Here are some things you can practice.

New Mindful Game Play: Choosing Next Actions

Question to ask yourself:

- What can I do in this situation that will move me toward a goal I prefer?

Actions I can practice:

- Be aware of the actions I am taking and if they support my goal or are fight/flight, looking for agreement, and gathering proof.
- Choose the actions that are aligned with my goal, despite how I may feel, even if that is to do nothing in that moment.

Strategy 4: Strategizing to Thrive—Facts and Data

Mabel also realized that when she was in survival mode, she had filtered out a lot of information that may have benefited her. Looking for more facts and data is useful when getting back to thriving.

Realize that when you are triggered, you are not seeing a full picture, that your vision and access to data has become limited. Looking for more information or another interpretation can aid you in making a good decision about what you should do next.

Have you ever gotten an e-mail that just made you mad, and so you quickly hit reply, with a response that told the other person how it really was? You were sure that it was articulate and to the point and that the point was very much what they would be getting. Then you pushed send with that "that will teach them" righteous feeling. You huffed and puffed for a couple of minutes, maybe went to get coffee, and then came back to your desk. You were calmer and breathing easier. You felt a little curious about how that person could have had the gall to send the e-mail, so you opened it up again and reread it.

You felt your face flush because in your first automatic reaction, you completely missed a key phrase that totally changed the meaning of the e-mail. The person wasn't putting up a barrier; they were saving the day.

I have had this happen before.

Seeing Red

When you feel yourself go into a negative emotion, if you are aware of how you are feeling, then you will be conscious of the fact that your alarm has been triggered because the situation is similar to a past situation that you determined was a danger. The trigger has more to do with the past then the present or the future. You fit the facts and data into your danger story. The current situation may not be the threat that it appears to be.

Now, you may not like what is happening. And the fact may be that what is happening is an obstacle to you moving toward your goal. So how you feel may be valid and understandable. You don't need to deny how you feel or start condemning that you are in survival mode. This just creates a new set of actions proving the enemy is wrong, but this time the perceived enemy is your emotions. It is the same trap.

If you feel triggered, name how you feel. It is valid. You will be acknowledging the alarm that was set off and know that you need to become more alert to the facts and data to see if there is really a danger and what the best action is to take.

Your emotional response is not the all-knowing seer of what is really happening; it is that smoke detector that has sensed a danger that you previously programmed. If you react in an automatic fight-or-flight way, you will then fall into the trap of proving that the danger was real, even if it was not. Your brain will see it as a need to survive. If you use the alarm to heighten your awareness and really look at the facts of the situation, you will be better able to determine the best course of action toward your goals.

Now, this is not always an easy thing to do. Sometimes we are so upset that we see red. It is hard to see or hear or believe that any other interpretation is possible. Again, this should be a signal to you that you are in survival mode. How you are feeling is creating the situation more than what is really happening. If you are aware, you have a choice. It may take willpower to look for more facts and not just gather more evidence to prove you are right. But it is a matter of having only two options (fight or flight) that are very limiting or having the possibility of many options that create a better outcome.

Seeking Support

If you choose getting back to thriving mode, one action that you can take, instead of calling a friend to tell your story and get agreement, is to call a trusted friend to tell your story so that he or she can give you a different interpretation and perspective.

When I am feeling frustration or worry, I find that when I tell my sisters or friends about the situation and what I am afraid it means, I am no longer looking for agreement. The last thing I want now is someone agreeing with how bad I feel things are or may be heading at the moment. I also am not looking for someone to just say, "It will be all right." My definition of the support that I want from others and give in return is that they acknowledge that I am capable and powerful enough to handle the situation, even if I do not believe it at the moment. Instead of joining me in worrying, they help me refocus on what I want and give me some alternative interpretations, questions to ask, or things to do that I may not be able to see. I no longer want them to join me in survival mode but to give me a hand to find my way back to thriving mode.

There are probably people you know, you may be one of them, that have a practice of having someone else read sensitive e-mails that they write when they are triggered before they send them out. And I think it would be another good practice to have someone neutral read the e-mail that upset you in the first place. This is a way of getting support in finding more facts and data.

Use this support to determine if there are facts that you are missing or may have filtered out that you need to inquire about, and what assumptions you are making that may not be true. This support can be a guide to help you refocus on your true goal, what you really want.

The more you practice getting out of survival mode, the more you will find that you don't want people to give you agreement that things are awful, because you know it doesn't help change the situation or move you toward your goal. You will know the people you can go to who will give you a broader perspective, along with suggesting options and solutions. This can be a trusted friend or a coach.

Your world changes when you let new data in and adjust your interpretation.

Mabel used four tools to help her move out of survival and make her way back to thriving. She paid attention to how she was feeling, and when she realized how frustrated and anxious she was, she examined what it was that she believed about the situation that was causing her to feel so bad. With the insight that she was afraid of failing and being seen as incompetent, she refocused her actions and attention to what was really important to her, to her goals of being a contributing employee to her coworkers and for her customers. This refocusing let her see a bigger picture, where she needed more information and feedback to make better decisions going forward, to see how she could improve her performance and her relationships.

Choosing to find more facts instead of going into fight or flight saved me a lot of stress one evening. I had made a trip to Chicago to meet with my new supervisor and team.

It was a short trip, and I had meetings scheduled for most of my time there. Since I had my smartphone, I didn't see a need to bring my laptop. In one of the meetings, my new director asked a question, and it came up that I had not brought my computer.

"Well, were you not planning to do any work on this trip?" she commented right before she left the room (a little sarcastically, it sounded to me).

This sent me right into survival mode.

I felt embarrassed and worried that I was not meeting expectations, and I was afraid she was thinking I was not up to standards with this situation. Were there any other expectations I was not meeting?

I could hear the dialogue in my head about how unfair she was being and that it was her fault for not communicating; I realized that I was recreating her as enemy number one. I did not want that to happen.

So the moment the meeting was over, I went right to her office and asked for more information. This conversation helped me understand that she wasn't seeing it as a big issue and had realized that she did not let me know that she expected all her managers to always travel with their laptops. I asked her if there were any other expectations that I needed to know about that I might not be meeting. She said no, that things were moving along well.

Because I knew that gathering more information would help to keep me from going further into survival mode, I was able to take the actions I needed to be a valued employee for this manager. It also saved me from a growing paranoia about my performance.

Putting It All Together

The great thing about a mindful game of thriving is that you can be deep in survival mode, and if you apply any of these strategies, it can pull you out and create a new world of possibilities.

I was asked to come in and share the Thriving beyond Survival model in a group's goal-setting session. The director and managers wanted to use the model to have their team members focus on the same goal as a group, see the goal as meaningful, and address beliefs that could distract them. They also wanted the model to allow the employees to ask for what they wanted and needed to be able to meet the goal—and to have it be fun.

There was another issue that was not addressed in the meeting but was a frustration for the managers. There was a group of employees who felt like they were promised promotions but that their managers were preventing them from getting the advancement they deserved. They felt entitled.

At a follow-up meeting about a month after the session, I reviewed the model and asked if any of the employees wanted to share how they had used it.

One of the most vocal of the complainers stood up and talked about how there was a day when she was on break and heard herself talking about how unfair it was that she was not getting promoted. In that moment, she realized that she was in survival mode, getting agreement and gathering evidence, and that as long as she was in that mode, she was never getting promoted.

She set up a meeting with her manager that day to get the facts about what she specifically needed to do to advance and was currently working on the criteria. She said she had not been this happy in her job in a long time.

Three months after that meeting, she was promoted and became one of the most optimistic employees in the department. Soon others followed, and within six months, over 13 percent of the employees had been promoted, and more were becoming qualified for promotion.

New Mindful Game Play: Facts/Data

Questions to ask yourself:

- What are the observable facts in this situation? What was said, done?
- What facts or data may I be missing that may give me a bigger picture or new perspective?
- Do I feel I am stuck with only two bad choices?
- Who can I ask that will give me the information that will allow me to make the most beneficial decision?

Actions to practice:

- Find someone you trust to give you a different perspective and options that will support you in progressing toward your goal.
- Be sure to let the person know you are not looking for agreement but for a clearer perspective.

Strategy 5: Staying in the Mindful Game with Appreciation

From now on, when you find yourself in survival mode, you will have four different strategies that you can use to move you back into thriving mode:

- Be aware of your emotions and what you are thinking and doing. When you find that you are in survival mode, you can choose to change your beliefs about the situation.
- Refocus on your goal and the outcomes you prefer rather than focusing on what you don't want.

- Make the choice of taking action toward your goals instead of finding proof and evidence that you can't have what you want.
- Seek the information you need to make decisions that will keep you moving toward your goal.

The first time that you consciously shift from survival mode into thriving mode and know that your world is different because of your change in perception and not an external change in the circumstances, you are truly empowered.

You will have shown yourself that it is possible to find your way to thriving. You will be more aware of the times you are triggered and fall into fight or flight, catch yourself sooner, and have the determination to refocus on what you really want and prefer.

When you are in thriving mode, you also have the opportunity to increase the time you spend there and have fewer situations knock you off balance and into survival mode. You can do this by cultivating the emotion of appreciation.

The key is in the *emotion* of appreciation.

Most of us realize that we should be grateful, count our blessings, and appreciate how good we really have it. But just being able to list what we know we appreciate does not have much of an impact on our well-being. It may even make us feel guilty that we are feeling negative emotions when we don't have it as bad as others—once again putting us in survival mode.

Cultivating the *emotion* of appreciation, on the other hand, allows us to see that we ourselves can create the positive emotions that we had been hoping to receive from a person or circumstance.

There are several benefits to cultivating this positive emotion. According to studies done by psychologist Barbara Fredrickson, positive emotions fuel psychological resilience, trigger upward spirals toward greater well-being in the future, and seeds human flourishing (Fredrickson, 2004). And Walter J. Freeman, a neuroscientist out of Berkeley, was the first to argue that there is a connection between love and appreciation and massive unlearning of old habits to allow for new ones to be created (Freeman, 1995).

So How Can You Cultivate this Feeling of Appreciation?

One way, as we talked about earlier in chapter 6, is by creating a habit of being mindful of what emotions you are feeling. This lets you be aware that you are feeling a negative emotion and may be going into survival mode. It also lets you be aware of when you are feeling positive emotions. And those moments when you are feeling positive, you can consciously appreciate the situation, who you are with, and yourself in the present moment.

Another practice is to take some time when you are at home and feel safe, maybe before you go to sleep or when you wake up, to think about someone or something that easily brings you that feeling of appreciation; it could be a loved one, a pet, a place, or an experience. When you are feeling that emotion, think of the people in your life and feel that same level of appreciation for them as human beings, especially the people you may see as enemies, people who have been your metaphorical tigers.

The moment you feel true appreciation for an enemy, that person is no longer an enemy but an opponent. This opens a whole new opportunity for dialogue that makes win/wins possible.

Also, practice feeling that same level of appreciation for *yourself*. Nurture and strengthen your belief that you are worthy to succeed.

No Enemies

A couple of years ago when I was totally miserable and in survival mode with my job, I became convinced that cultivating appreciation was a powerful and effective technique.

The vice president of our area was one of those leaders that seemed to take pleasure in pulling the rug out from under you. He could be called a bully.

A year earlier, he had reorganized the department and let go of all but one member of my team of five without consulting me—and I was their manager. Then he reorganized again and let go of my director and had me reporting to a different director in a totally different department.

He was my enemy.

Any time I would get a call, e-mail, or even think about him, I would tense up and get anxious and upset.

I was tired of being paranoid and stressed out and decided I would give this appreciation thing a try. So I did the practice I just described every night before I went to sleep.

I would first think about my nephews, because I can't help but feel the warm emotion of love and appreciation when I think about them. I decided that this was the level of appreciation I would use as my baseline and had a goal to experience the same level of appreciation when I thought about my VP. I couldn't just jump to that same intensity, so I went to an easier target next and felt that level of appreciation for my coworkers and worked my way up to the VP.

It was hard at first because I would tense up any time I thought about this guy, but I told myself that I just needed to relax and hold the sense of appreciation for him for a few minutes, and he would never need to know.

And after a few nights of practicing this, I was actually able to get there. I was able to feel authentic appreciation for the VP as a person. In that moment, this VP was no longer my enemy I needed to fight or avoid. I was able to view him more as an opponent in my mindful game of thriving.

I also cultivated that same level of appreciation for myself. It had me build my sense of worthiness and capability.

I really saw the effect of doing this practice when the VP called me up to tell me that he was moving me to another department, one that I had no expertise in and under another new director. The reason he gave for the move was that I was in Texas, and this new manager was in Texas, and so this should make me happy. This did not make me happy, and it was not something I would have chosen for myself.

I found myself doing something I had never done before: I started to speak up for myself and what I wanted, and I was doing it in a way that was respectful. I told him that it was not a situation that I was happy with and that assuming that he knew how I would feel about it did not show respect for my viewpoint.

I would not have done that before practicing appreciation. It didn't change the situation, but it did change how I perceived the situation. And it changed my relationship with the VP. He left me alone for the most part, and the only time he got in contact with me was to ask my opinion, which he had never done before. And in a few months, he was let go.

I can now honestly say that there is nobody in my life that I see as an enemy. And this is so freeing.

Another practice that helps to create a focus on appreciation is to keep a daily journal of the things that you appreciated during the day. This lets your unconscious brain know that finding things to appreciate is a priority, and it will set up a filter to look for positive things that are happening around you.

Many people defend their worry as a way of protecting themselves from what can go wrong, and many people are afraid that if they let go of their negative filter, they may get blindsided.

Having a filter for the positive and being in thriving mode does not mean that you won't be aware of when things are not going the way that you would like or need them to go. What it will do is increase your resilience so that when you feel things taking a wrong turn, you are able to view a bigger picture, see more options, look for creative solutions, and take actions that will keep you on track with your goals.

You will find that you have the courage to use your authentic voice to stand up for yourself and your beliefs with respect for the other person and their perspective and beliefs.

Fully Experience Appreciation

Cultivating appreciation is a practice that will transform your life. And when I say appreciation, I mean the emotion of appreciation, not just the idea of appreciation. You cannot be in survival mode and experience the emotion of appreciation.

You may be able to say that you appreciate (or respect, love, etc.) your enemy because you know you do when you are calm or because you know you are supposed to, but you need to understand that when you are in survival mode, in that moment, you are not appreciating (respecting, loving, etc.) the other person no matter how many times you say you are. It does not matter who your enemy is at the moment—your child, your spouse, yourself. When we are in fight or flight, there is no room for appreciation.

There are many people out there that claim they love everybody— yet "those people over there still have to die" or be punished or should lose. That is not appreciation or love.

When we are in appreciation, we are more able to hold people accountable, because we see them as capable. We don't need to make them proof that we are right about how people are.

We are able to give feedback that makes a difference. Because it is not about making someone wrong or judging them, it is truly about giving the other person information that will help them stay on track or course-correct toward their goals. People love and crave that type of information. They do not love or even listen well to opinions and judgments about how badly or wrong they are doing things.

Appreciate Yourself

When you are in appreciation and thriving, you can leave a situation that is not working because you appreciate yourself and know that you deserve to be in a situation that allows you to move toward your goal. And you can leave without needing to be bitter or resentful. You can also decide to stay to see what you can learn and if you can influence the situation because it aligns with what you want and who you are, not because you feel obligated or locked in as a victim.

There is a difference between standing up *for* yourself and standing up *to* someone else. When you stand up for yourself, you are speaking your truth about what is working or not working for you and asking for what you need. When people stand up to someone else, it is usually to prove that they are right and the other person is wrong, and it comes from a sense of being a victim.

People complain to their friend about how unfair their boss has been, looking for agreement and allies to their case, fighting the good fight of being shown respect, and their friend will tell the complainer that he or she needs to go stand up to that boss and give him or her a piece of their mind. This is a fight tactic, spouting all the complaints to an enemy of how they are doing them wrong and being unfair. Telling them off good.

You may have done this, and it may feel good in the moment because of our sick glee of righteousness; we just proved our case, so we feel right, but all we end up with is making someone else feel bad so that we can feel good.

And if the other person apologizes to calm you down, and even if they take it as getting good feedback and information, you are still weighed down by your belief that you can't have what you want, and it was that person's fault. You feel that you have gained ground, but you are still waiting for a similar situation to use as proof. Usually, the other person gets defensive, and instead of getting an apology, you get a bigger fight and more proof of how wrong things are, along with a damaged relationship.

On the other hand, when in thriving, you don't see the value in standing up to someone, criticizing them, and making them feel bad for something that did not work or became an obstacle for you. And you don't just allow people to walk all over you either.

When in thriving mode, you not only appreciate other people, but you have appreciation for yourself too. You are able to talk to people about what works and doesn't work for you, but it is coming from speaking up for yourself and a belief that you deserve to be treated in a respectful manner, not from needing to attack someone who did not treat you well.

You are able to ask for what you need and feel as though you deserve it, all the while letting the other person decide how he or she will respond. Their response will not be a reflection of you but a reflection of themselves. Many times, we may feel an impact of an action and interpret it as intentional or mean-spirited, but when we describe what happened and how we felt about it as feedback, we find that the other person didn't intend to have the impact he or she did.

We are more powerful when we are coming from truly appreciating the people and situations around us, especially when we are appreciating ourselves. When we are in appreciation and thriving, we don't need to prove anything; we already know we deserve what we want, and we can have what we want; we only need to take appropriate action.

When we are in appreciation and thriving, we are our own best friend. We are our biggest support.

Mabel started to feel better and more balanced when she focused on getting her productivity back to the high standards that she was used to. She scheduled a meeting with her supervisor and went into the discussion with an intention to share her professional goals, build a better relationship, and learn what his vision and expectations were. The conversation seemed a bit awkward at first, but she kept focused, and by the end of the meeting, both of them were aligned on measuring the progress toward the goals of the department. Mabel was no longer in survival mode; she was back to thriving and excited about what she was set to accomplish with her team.

Here are some practices to cultivate your emotion of appreciation.

New Mindful Game Play: Cultivate the Emotion of Appreciation

- When you feel good, consciously appreciate what is going on and who is with you.
- When in a safe place, practice appreciating your enemies and turn them into opponents.
- Appreciate yourself.
- Keep an appreciation journal.

You now have a set of strategies that with practice will get you back to thriving faster and allow you to stay there longer, no matter what the situation. By noticing when you are in survival and refocusing on what it is you really want, getting all the facts, and being conscious that your next action is toward your goal, soon you will start to see your time in survival mode become shorter and shorter, and your time in thriving become more your norm.

But what about the people around you? What happens when they are in survival mode? How do you not let it get you out of your mindful game of thriving?

CHAPTER 7

When Others Are in a Different Game

I had someone once ask me, "But, Martha, what if someone is *really* out to get you?"

And that may be a fact; you may be considered an enemy to someone who is in survival mode and is gathering evidence to get you. It may not be your intention to be an enemy, but there you are; you are their proverbial tiger.

You now have a choice. Do you deal with this situation in thriving mode or in survival mode?

If you approach it from survival mode, you have a fight on your hands. It is now hero against villain. You are set against them in a fight with a winner and a loser, and neither will tolerate being a loser. So the situation will more likely escalate, both sides building their cases, gathering allies, each trying to destroy the other. This may be all done in a professional and politically correct manner, but the chance of the situation getting better or anything being solved is very low. Remember, when in survival, you are not really looking for a solution; you are looking for proof that you are right.

If you deal with the situation while in thriving mode, there are more options and opportunities. For one thing, you don't need to see the other person as an enemy nor yourself as a victim; the other person becomes more of an opponent in your mindful game. You will not be focused on beating them; you will be focused on what your goal is in the situation, both short-term and long-term.

Because the other person is not an enemy, you will be interested in what it is that the person wants and why he or she is seeing you as an enemy. You may not be able to change the person's mind, but you will be able to understand where he or she is coming from. You are more open to listening to his or her interpretation of what happened and what you may have done to make him or her feel threatened. With this information, you have an opportunity to provide resolution and look for solutions, all the while appreciating him or her as a human being and how he or she may have interpreted the situation.

This does not mean you agree with the person, and it does not mean that you will let the person have his or her way just to keep the peace. You may decide to do things that may upset the person more, but the actions will not be to prove him or her wrong. Your actions will be to move you and the other person closer to a more beneficial place.

When you are in thriving, your main focus is what actions are going to be most effective in moving you toward what you want. And it may be that you need to break off a relationship or leave a situation, not as a reaction but as a decision. To break a cycle or pattern. To be able to accomplish your goals.

A Common Trap

Many of the struggles and conflicts that escalate into major fights, disagreements, or wars may be due to the widespread belief that we have to get others to do things they don't want to do in order for us to get what we want. This belief derails our focus from our goal. We put more time and effort in finding ways to make someone take an action rather than looking for other solutions or options. And when we find any resistance coming from the other person, we end up making him or her an enemy because that person is keeping us from what we want. We find we are in a battle with people who we care about and want to be on the same team with, whether it is our family members, coworkers, or students.

How to Elude the Trap

To avoid falling into this common trap, it is important to let go of the belief that you have to make people do things or that others have to behave in a certain way for you to feel comfortable or be in thriving. From your own experience, you know you have more energy when you are doing something that you feel personally aligned with and resent being *made* to do something by somebody, no matter what it is, and it is exhausting to try to behave exactly how others want us to behave; there are too many out there that have different expectations.

Be clear about what your goal is, what it is you want, and your belief in the benefit of the intended outcome, and find others who are willing to opt in to help make it happen. Allowing people to opt in has their focus and actions aligned with the same goal as you.

When you share a vision for what you are passionate about and believe in, your actions are consistent, and you have a group of people opt in because the vision is consistent with what they want for themselves, that's being a leader.

Don't Get Sucked into Someone Else's Drama

There may be times when you are in thriving mode, and someone you are interacting with is having a bad day and is looking for agreement that his or her life is not going well.

I was probably eleven years old that Saturday, playing at the side of the house with my younger brother Eddie.

We were just getting the scenario down for our game of secret agents when my mom came out of the house, screen door slamming, her stern voice enunciating each word. "You do not have permission to be outside! You need to go right back in this house and up to your room."

I felt the anger rolling off my mom and saw the look of terror in my brother's eyes. I felt blindsided because I had no clue as to what we had done wrong, but by the tone in my mom's voice, I knew she wasn't open to a Q&A.

I followed my brother into the house, up the stairs, and then veered toward the room I shared with my sister Ginny after watching Eddie go into the room he shared with our brother Timmy.

I flopped down on my bed and leaned against the wall, feeling the tension at the back of my throat and the threat of tears. I had to have done something awful to be in that much trouble, so I reviewed the morning and the evening before in my head, going over everything I had done to see where my error lay. Whenever I found out what I did, I was not going to do it again.

About forty-five minutes later, Ginny came into the room, excited about the gossip she got to tell me.

"Eddie got grounded this morning for skipping his chores yesterday, and this afternoon he snuck out and got caught by mom when she got back from the grocery store. Boy is he in deep trouble now."

"Really? Wow," I said. I felt embarrassed by the fear and guilt I had felt, because none of this situation had anything to do with me. I felt the emotions of anger from my mom and fear from my brother. I became part of their drama.

Being social beings, when someone is in survival mode and fearful, we pick up on what they are feeling, and if we are not paying attention, we may start to prepare for the danger and look for the stories that fit the emotions that we are picking up on. This ability to sense others' emotions was needed for the survival of the tribe. When there was a danger coming at the settlement, you wanted everyone to act quickly, not question or doubt but to get ready to fight off the attack from the enemy or flee the overflowing river. When it was life or death, that reaction saved not just the person who saw the danger first but the person's whole family.

In a situation when people feel fear that their idea is not being heard or their position is in danger, and they go into fight or flight, if you are not aware of your own emotions and mindful of what is going on, you may join them in their survival reaction, sign on as an ally and prepare to fight the enemy or flee the scene, when all the while the danger has nothing to do with you.

Throughout your day, you interact with any number of people, from family at home and close coworkers in the office to strangers in line for a movie, all having a different perspective and reaction to the situation and people around them. Some will be focused on the options and solutions to the news that the movie they came to see just sold out, while others may be looking for agreement on how horribly the management team is handling the divisional reorganization.

If you are not mindful of what you want from the situation and your own reactions, you may end up going with the flow of the mood of the other people in the situation—either getting on the bandwagon when someone else is upset, or contributing to a brainstorming session when others are looking for solutions, never aware that you have a choice.

This transfer of emotion is documented in Howard Friedman and Ronald Riggio's research, "Effect of Individual Differences in Nonverbal Expressiveness on Transmission of Emotions" (Friedman & Riggio, 1981). Their studies found that when three strangers sit facing each other in silence for a minute or two, the one who is most emotionally expressive transmits his or her mood to the other two, without speaking a single word.

In the example with my brother, I felt the tension and fear and was looking for how my story fit the emotions of the situation and reacting as if the emotions were mine.

After creating the model and applying it to my own life, I realized that I was still reacting to not only my own but other people's fear and anxiety and stress as if those emotions were mine. When my friend was feeling anxious but wasn't talking about the issue, I would feel anxious and then worry about things at work or in my family that had not been bugging me before. My mind would look for something in my own story that would fit the emotion I was feeling so that it would make some sense to me, even if my unconscious had to hide some holes in the logic.

Only when I paid attention to how I was feeling did I notice that some of my anxiety was not originating from me but from the people around me; I was just in the habit of claiming the emotion as mine.

I remember one of the first times I was consciously aware of this empathy.

I was at my desk working on a big project that was going to get a lot of exposure in the organization. The conversation I just had with Carol in the communication and graphics area was energizing. We had brainstormed ideas on how to approach the internal marketing, and I was rolling the ideas over in my head, feeling the flow of the creative process.

My phone rang.

"Hi, Martha. I need to know if you have some time to work on a PowerPoint that we are preparing for the meeting with the senior leadership. I got it started but would like you to proof and edit." My boss, Alice, sounded calm, but I began to feel a bit panicky.

This was a very different feeling from the one I had just a second ago. Maybe she had sent an e-mail earlier, and I missed it, so she was about to scold me about not replying. I scrolled through my inbox, but there was nothing there from my boss.

"Sure. I should have some time this afternoon to work on it. When do you need it back?" I replied.

She continued to give me directions for what she needed from me and even thanked me in advance. Why was I feeling so incompetent and as if I needed to prepare myself for some bad news or negative feedback? And the longer we were on the phone, the more anxious I felt.

She said good-bye with no "oh and by the way" blindsiding comment, and we hung up.

As I put down the phone, I took a deep breath. With such strong feelings, my first thought was to jump on the task requested before I got into the trouble that my emotions had been screaming I was already in. Instead, I took a moment to not act but to really pay attention to the emotions to see what they were about. To my amazement, instead of feeling the worry build, I felt the wave of negativity fade away and the previous excitement and flow I had felt about the project I was working on come back.

It was at that moment that I realized the emotions I was feeling on the phone call were not mine or even about me, that every word my boss said was respectful and supportive. The anxiety must have been hers. I also knew that if I had not stopped and paid attention, I would have found justification for the emotions I felt on the phone, and my afternoon would have been miserable. I breathed a sigh of relief.

Later that afternoon, when I was going over the edited slides with Alice, I found out that just before our earlier call, she had been in a meeting in which her boss had strongly criticized her and her work. She hadn't mentioned the meeting because she did not want to upset me.

You are sensitive to the emotions of the people around you. If you are unaware of these emotions, you may fall into fight or flight for situations that may have otherwise been inconsequential.

You get a phone call from your mother who is worried about her money situation, and you find that you are in a bad mood for the rest of the day. And when someone asks you why, you blame it on your mother and complain about how she doesn't listen to you and is a moocher and look for agreement on how wrong she is to drag you into her problems. The mood spreads. You are in survival mode too.

☞ Be aware of how news that you get from TV, Facebook, or other sources affects how you feel, and be mindful of if you are claiming negative emotions that are not even yours. Adding your fear and anger to a larger group of others who are afraid and angry will not increase the chances of a solution. As we have learned, it does quite the opposite.

Instead, play a mindful game of the possibility of a solution you prefer and take actions that move you in that direction in your own life.

What If I Find Myself Drawn into the Drama?

I have a friend, I'll call Karen, who had a roommate complain about a mutual friend of theirs whom the roommate also worked with. The roommate described how the other friend was totally disrespectful in their interactions at work, and things got so bad that the roommate actually lost her job.

Karen was aware that her roommate was in survival mode and attempted to help her get back to thriving through the situation, but the more she heard about the story, the more disappointed she became with the other friend. Karen was aware that she had heard only one side of the story but believed there was enough evidence to know that the other friend's behavior was totally unacceptable. She was so sure that she totally lost respect for a friend that she had otherwise enjoyed being with. Even though Karen understands the Thriving beyond Survival model, she still got herself trapped in survival mode, being right that her friend was wrong. Without intending, she had made her friend an enemy in a situation that she was not even directly involved in.

What Karen is finding hard to see is that her negative emotions are not only about the other person's behavior but about a specific belief that there is something she really wants, and this situation is proof that she is right that she can't have it. It may be the belief that women should support other women and that people should respect other people, which are both good values. This situation is a valid example where neither of those things is happening, so her feelings of disappointment are valid. However, the negative emotions Karen is feeling are indications that the situation has her in survival mode, and she is being distracted from what it is she really wants. Despite all the other positive interactions she had in the past, Karen is using this one situation to totally paint her friend as a bad person whom she does not want to associate with, and if she did confront her, she would want to have the other person know that she is wrong and should feel bad, neither of which sounds supportive or respectful.

☞ What can you do if you find yourself in a similar situation and want to get back to thriving, back to feeling good and focusing on what you want instead of blaming someone else for keeping you from it?

Here are some things my friend and you can try:

- Become *aware* of how you are feeling and realize that being upset is an indication that something that you want to happen is not happening, and you are in survival mode.
- Acknowledge and write down the emotions you feel; they may be disappointment, frustration, anger, despair, or other negative feelings.
- Write down what it is that you want that you are afraid that you can't have. In my friend's case, it may be that people in her life, especially women, respect each other. For you, it may be that you want to be able to trust people, to be valued, to be respected, to be successful.
- Notice that you are seeing the other person as an enemy and blaming him or her for how you feel. Ask yourself if thinking about the person either has you wanting to yell (fight) or avoid them as much as possible (flight).

- Acknowledge that you are in survival mode and that it is a valid place to be. Then ask yourself if you want to spend your time going through the evidence of being right and being justified that this situation is proof that you can't have what you want or if you want to get back to thriving.
- Choose.

If you choose thriving:

- As was described in chapter 6, write down emotions that you would rather feel about the situation, the other person, and yourself.

Example: I want to feel appreciation, compassion, confident.

- Write down goals that you prefer for you, your relationship with the other person, and the situation.

Example: I want people to respect each other. I want to support and be supported by people in my life.

- Write down that facts of what you saw or heard and what you have made it mean.

Example: I was told that she accused my roommate of being dishonest. I made it mean that she was a mean and disrespectful person who had me duped into believing that she was nice. I made it mean that I was wrong for trusting her.

- Decide if you need more facts to get a broader picture or to get support in seeing a different perspective.
- Take actions that are aligned with the goals you created and prefer in the situation, as opposed to getting agreement, finding proof, or fight/flight.

- Practice the exercise of cultivating the emotion of appreciation for the other person as a human being. When you are coming from true appreciation, you are able to give people feedback on behavior that doesn't work or that you know is not aligned with what they truly want, and it will be to give the other person useful information, not proof of how wrong he or she is. You will be able to have a conversation to get to understanding and move in a win/win direction.

It takes a conscious shift in focus to go from a feeling of being right about someone back to thriving mode, but the feeling of freedom you get is worth it, and it becomes easier the next time.

Influence of Emotions—It Works Both Ways

Your thriving has a wider impact than you can anticipate.

As much as negative emotions from other people who are in survival mode can be contagious, the positive emotions of thriving are also a powerful influence.

A study at the Yale University School of Management found that among working groups, cheerfulness and warmth spread most easily, while irritability is less contagious, and depression spreads hardly at all (Barsade & Gibson, 1998).

Shining the Light on the Path to Thriving for Someone Else

Those times during your day-to-day progress toward your goal, when you find that you are interacting with someone who is in survival mode and has a limited view of the situation, you may be wondering how you can use what you know about thriving beyond survival to support the person.

Below are some hints on how to interact with that person to keep the focus on the goal for the person and for you.

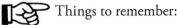 Things to remember:

- **Remember to feel genuine appreciation for other people and where they are.** If you are able to feel appreciation, you will not see them as enemies and will have the capacity to have patience and compassion for where they are. You will also be able to be curious as to their point of view. You will be able to ask inquiring questions and not try to prove that they are wrong.

- **Remember that there is nothing wrong with being in survival mode.** This is very human. Their danger alarm has been triggered. What will help them feel safe? Being able to understand the threat they feel and why from their point of view will enable you to show empathy. When most people are angry or upset, what they want most is to be heard. This does not mean you have to agree with them. You just need to let them know that you respect their point of view enough to understand where they are coming from. You can also discover what is important to them so that you can help them to feel safe.

- **Remember to attempt to support someone who is in survival only when you are in thriving mode.** If you feel upset or negative emotions that have someone seeming to be an enemy, it may be more productive to step back and take a breather so that you can get refocused on your goal and get back to thriving mode. If you interact with someone in survival mode while you yourself are in survival mode, what you have is a fight, a lose/lose situation, because both of you will be fighting to be right so that the other person is wrong. If one of you is in thriving, the possibility of a win/win increases exponentially.

- **Remember: you can't do it for them.** You cannot get anyone out of survival mode and into thriving mode but yourself; you can only offer support and guidance. Be compassionate toward them and yourself. If they are not able to calm down, reschedule the conversation.

Actions you can take:

- **Listen.** Sometimes listening with empathy or compassion (and not agreement) allows others to vent and then find their way back to thriving. It will also let you know what the best questions may be to ask to support them out of survival mode and into thriving mode.
- **Ask if they would like support.** If the other person is only wanting agreement and not ready to look for a solution toward his or her goal or a mutual goal, give the person some space and time. He or she will not be able to see the options that you may be able to see. People will fight for their limitations when they are in survival mode because it is about being right that they can't have what they want, and it's the other person's fault. And as we saw in the previous chapters, they will believe that they are fighting the good fight, so they will be more focused on proof and evidence. It may be more effective to wait for a time when they are not triggered to lend support in finding options.
- **Ask Inquiring questions and give feedback on what you hear.** If they are open to support and finding a solution, you can ask inquiring questions to give you more information on the situation and their perspective. Some good questions to ask are:

  ○ What is their goal? What do they want in the situation (ultimately)?
  ○ What is their concern/fear/belief?

○ What are the facts of the situation? What was said and done, without the interpretation?

- **Offer other interpretations.** Once you know the facts and if they are open to support, you can offer other interpretations that may be more empowering for them and give them more options. You may also help them see opportunity for more data gathering. (Remember you are in thriving mode and will see a fuller picture. In the end, they will need to choose their interpretation and actions to take.)
- **Refocus them on what it is they are really wanting—their goal.**
- **Give them space and time.**
- **Be a role model. Take actions that are consistent with your goals.**

Whatever mindful game you create, you will have others around you who will either be aligned with the goal you are progressing toward or may feel to you like an opponent or obstacle that can have you be curious and creative. Take the perspective that he or she is playing a particular role and that your job is never to *make* him or her do something, especially something that the person doesn't want to do. You best support others by being an example for the power of aligning your own beliefs and actions with the goal you prefer and supporting them in their own alignment.

To make a difference in the lives of the people in your life is to thrive, and with the best games, there are endless ways to reach new and exciting levels in your life that you may never have imagined. In the next chapter, we will look at what can be available the longer you play your mindful game of thriving.

CHAPTER 8

Continuously Leveling Up

I freeze. My mind is blank, and I can't remember the words I am supposed to speak next. It is my final rehearsal for a talk to be videotaped before a live audience. I rehearsed this with no problem the day before, but at this moment, in front of the TEDx Fayetteville committee, I can't even find a thread toward my message.

My mouth is dry, so I take a sip of water. I try joking with the people who are there to give me feedback. They have concerned faces, though they try to be encouraging. Nothing is working. It is the third time at this spot in the presentation that I have drawn a blank.

I am bombing.

It is ironic to be in a situation where you are speaking about how to thrive in life, and your body, mind, and emotions are, at that moment, totally in survival mode.

Finally, I get back on track with the words that I have memorized and do my best to just get through to the end. I don't think I've smiled once. This is definitely an experience I would put in the failure column.

It was the best thing that could have happened.

Because I had been playing my mindful game of thriving for a while, I found that even though my body was in fight-or-flight mode, and I was feeling emotions like embarrassment, panic, and frustration, I quickly let it all go and found myself easily refocusing on my goal. I didn't ignore the emotions and chatter that were in my head; I listened and took note to gain insight into the beliefs that were being triggered. I also listened more closely to the feedback I was getting from the committee. I knew that I needed information to improve what obviously was a presentation that not only wasn't working for this audience but for me either.

In the past, having this reaction would have had me shut down in the moment. I would have heard little of the suggestions given and spent more of my time justifying or defending myself. I would have explained how I was worried about the time limit, which distracted me. I would have told myself that the committee members were being judgmental and therefore were not a good audience. I would have felt superior because I was one of the only speakers so far who actually didn't read their presentation, and so I had done more preparation. I would have used all of those thoughts to try to make me feel better, and it all would have distracted me from the information I could actually use to move me toward my intended goal.

But there was no strong pull to make the excuses. It did not take a strength of will to refocus myself on what I really wanted, which was to speak my message of thriving and to have fun doing it. I was able to feel the true strength of my well-practiced habit of choosing thriving by refocusing on what was truly important to me. I heard new chatter in my head that was telling me that I was going to gain a new insight that would let me release beliefs that were not beneficial to me. I felt myself looking forward to the moment I got fully back into thriving mode and how good that would feel. Even in the midst of feeling extremely uncomfortable, I was fully conscious that this moment of being in survival mode was truly temporary and not my norm.

I felt myself reach a new level of playing in my mindful game of thriving.

At this new level, there is an ability to feel the negative emotions of being in survival mode and still be open to information around me. I understand now what it means to not be afraid of being afraid. This understanding lets me trust myself to succeed even when I am experiencing failure. I listen and become conscious of previously unconscious beliefs. And what is even more exciting is that I know there will always be new levels for me to reach.

One of the things that game designers have discovered in creating their products is that players continue to play when they have the ability to level up. Leveling up happens when an individual's skills reach a mastery for the current level. Because thriving is about growing, we want to find more ways to grow our skills, and in games, this is done by moving to a new level that has more difficult challenges that enable us to continue to do new things and grow our skills. I personally like getting to a new level of capability and the availability of new opportunities with new levels when I play a video game, and I find that I experience this same joy of discovery in my mindful games of thriving.

The difference between a mindful game and a video game is that leveling up is not only about growing skills but about uncovering and letting go of unbeneficial beliefs. Both these accomplishments allow for new opportunities and behaviors.

When I felt frustration around being bullied by my boss but applied the model and was able to let go of that fear and having to prove that I was right, I reached a new level in my perspective and had options for behavior that allowed me to be more productive and focused on the goals I had that were important to me. I also found new things to pursue that seemed fun.

For instance, soon after that period of time, I put together presentations to groups on the concepts of the Thriving beyond Survival model. And in the years since, I have started my own company, written this book, and started building my own clientele. This is a totally new and exciting game for me, with its own challenges to which I have applied the concepts of the model. I continue to enjoy new experiences and not fall into the pitfalls of anxiety and stress for any length of time that I was told starting a new business creates.

When talking with people about leaving my current job and creating my own company, many of them asked if I was scared. This is an interesting question to ask someone who is willingly setting out into the unknown. Though they were supportive, the question was focused on not only the possibility but probability of my being predominantly in survival mode. This may have been due to either those people's own fear of pursuing their own business or what they have heard about starting a company.

I noticed that when I was asked that question, because I was choosing to stay focused on the dream I had, not only was I able to assure them that I was not fearful, but they couldn't help but notice my excitement. I was also aware that if I shifted my focus just even a little bit, I could easily generate a feeling of fear and anxiety and stop myself dead in my tracks. But I liked being excited more.

And it was not like there weren't any beliefs popping up that could distract me. I noticed that when I told people about my plans, there was a part of me waiting for that one person to tell me that I was crazy and it was a bad idea and I should not even attempt it. I never ran into that person; everyone I spoke with was fully supportive. And though I was aware of the belief, I did not give it much of my attention. I was able to see it as a belief I could choose and not the truth.

These experiences let me see that that there is always the choice of focusing on thriving or surviving. Each perspective is as valid as the other, but they have the potential of two very different experiences and outcomes. I choose every day how I want to focus.

When you practice applying the model and increase the times you choose to thrive instead of survive, you will see, as I have, that it takes less effort and energy to thrive than to be in survival mode.

It takes more effort to maintain a grudge and build a case against an enemy than it does to fulfill any of the dreams you may have—not only physically, because when we are in survival mode, our bodies are tense, our breath shallow, and our senses in overdrive, but also because our constant focus on what we don't want increases stress and uses a lot of our energy in order to always be on guard. We have been convinced that this is necessary in order to survive, and we have not stepped back to see what we are really afraid of. Many of us do not encounter a threat of physical danger, so the fear is more around what we believe things mean.

Model of Competition

In the Western world, the culture emphasizes competition. You may always be battling with someone or something for what you want or need, whether for money, for love, for grades, or position. So many of us have decided that our worth is measured by whether we are seen as a winner. And in a culture of competition, there is always a winner and a loser. This is another valid model of how we can experience the world that is out there similar to the victim, villain, hero model we talked about earlier.

A mindful game allows you to change your belief that competition is necessary to evolve, that in order to be worthy, you need to beat someone or something to get what you want, and that your only other alternative is losing.

There is an alternative view that may allow us to not only thrive but also to increase our levels of happiness—the belief in the power of cooperation and collaboration. Through cooperation, we may not only be more productive and create things beyond what we can now imagine and hence level up, but it may also be more natural for us as human beings.

Studies have found that whether a person's self-esteem is linked to competition or to cooperation is influenced by the culture he or she is raised in, not on inherent qualities. The belief of what is valued is what determines behaviors, not because it is or is not human nature (Fehr & Schmidt, 1999) (Kagan & Knight, 1979).

There are studies showing that cooperation is more pleasurable than competition and that we are far more productive and are able to learn quicker when we are immersed in an environment that values cooperation (Beersma, Hollenbeck, Humphrey, Moon, Conlon, & Iigen, 2003) (Deutsch, 1949) (Huayao & Xiaokun, 2011) (Kohn, 1986). We are also able to evaluate the cost to others of what we create or produce and make decisions in a more holistic mode. And this makes sense when you think about it. Don't you feel safer when you are working together with a team toward a goal than you do when you are pitted against each other and may be seen as a loser?

I am not saying that we need to get rid of competition. Competition is not bad or invalid either; it has been shown to increase the speed of what gets done. There is value in the thrill of getting something done fast or winning a race.

Competition, in the spirit of a game with a strong opponent, also lets us hone our skills and come up with new strategies because the growth and creativity is what excites us as much as winning. When winning isn't confused with our identity or worthiness, it becomes a means for us to see how much we have grown and what skills we want to build next.

But when competition is seen as the only valid way to prosper or be seen as good enough, as has been the case with Western society, it is less of a game and more about survival. Instead of opting into a competition because it excites us, we are forced into a constant grind of having to beat the competition. We see what may have been respected opponents as reviled enemies. We are constantly comparing where we are in life with the person next to us. If someone is doing well, we find it hard to be happy for the person because we believe that there is less chance for our success, or that we must be doing something wrong and he or she is better than us.

And in a belief that competition is the way of the world, instead of learning from our losses, we do everything we can to not be labeled a loser. We are exhausted, and though we have been told this is life and living, we are no longer thriving.

I believe that how things are in our Western American society has less to do with natural selection and survival of the fittest and more with the belief that this is life. Society wasn't and isn't created by one person or government; it is created by the cumulative effects of what each individual chooses to believe, whether people are aware they have that choice or not. I affect the world by what I choose to believe. And by choosing a world where I no longer have enemies and can appreciate and respect any opponents and even see them as friends, I find that I can remove myself from the belief that it is all about competition, and I can be cooperative in what I do.

Not having to be on the alert to an enemy around every corner does not mean that I leave myself vulnerable or blindly trusting. As you have learned by having gone through the model, it is the exact opposite. I am better able to see a clearer picture. If I do feel a tingling of fear or apprehension, I am able to keep my focus on what is most important at the moment, become aware of all the facts of the situation, and take action that is more appropriate to what is actually happening as opposed to what I am afraid may be happening.

Opportunity for Leveling Up

This doesn't mean that we may not find ourselves from time to time in survival mode or facing things that we don't prefer. It is part of being a live human being. We never want to be rid of an effective alarm system that alerts us to a danger, even if it is only a perceived one.

I use the concepts of the model every day, and I am amazed at what I have been able to accomplish, the relationships I have gained, and the overall fun I am having in my life. It is so much more than what it was before, and it excites me to know that there will always be a leveling up where life becomes even better than I have imagined.

When I first started to apply the model with my situation at work, when I saw most clearly that things were shifting for the better were those times when something would happen that would have upset me in the past, but now I perceived it only as a mild annoyance or even a nonissue.

At first, it was small things, like being given tasks that were not part of my role that I described earlier, to being passed over for a promotion even though I had more experience and qualifications. When I stayed in my mindful game of making a difference for the people I work for and with, I let neither of the situations distract me for long and actually found myself growing stronger in creating the unique and specific difference that I know I make.

Where I am profoundly grateful for having the model to use in my life was in the last year and a half of my dad's life.

That choice of making each moment with my dad special opened the door for having appreciation and love for him flow, no matter what the conditions. I did not feel frustration or anger with him when the daycare activity center he went to called me at work to tell me that he had gotten out and into the street and wouldn't come back inside—that I needed to come pick him up. I was able to handle the situation easily and work with my family to find options to help with his care.

There was one occasion where my mom called me because my dad was upset and angry, indicating that there was someplace he needed to be, and he kept walking out of the house. My mom had to go get him and bring him back in, and she was getting worn out, and he was getting more upset. She called to get some relief, so I went and picked him up and drove him around the area; this usually helped to calm him down. When he still seemed upset, I decided to stop and get us a cherry limeade at Sonic, something I knew he liked. I had to keep locking the doors to keep him from getting out of the car.

None of my usual distractions for him were working, and because I was not falling into survival mode and getting frustrated or anxious, I was able to keep focusing on having my time with him be special no matter what was happening. I was able to come up with other ideas.

I took him back to my house and had him come inside. He walked in grudgingly, with his arms folded and a stern look. My dad had crystal blue eyes that could pierce you with icicles when he was in a mood.

Knowing my dad loved music, I connected my iPod to the speakers and pushed play. When the music came on, I started to dance. I looked over at my dad and saw him nodding his head to the music, then moving his feet, and it wasn't too long before he was smiling. The next song came on, and we both danced. I found a tambourine and gave it to him, and he was laughing with joy. We danced for over twenty minutes.

Playing a mindful game of thriving made that potentially difficult and draining situation into one of the most special and moving times I spent with my dad.

Figure 14: Martha and Joseph Germann
(Photograph by Virginia Germann)

When my dad died, I felt no regret for having not appreciated the time I spent with him. I was at peace with our relationship. This is a huge blessing.

An added benefit of forming and focusing on my goal of special time with my dad also altered my relationship with my mom. In my mindful game with my dad, I no longer needed a tiger to fight against and so no longer had any tendency to see my mom as an enemy. I was able to feel and grow my appreciation for her. My relationship with her gets better and better the more we are both playing a mindful game of thriving.

When my dad's condition began manifesting, I could have chosen to feel resentful for my dad's disease, upset with the doctors for not doing more, upset with my mom for not doing better, or upset with myself and the rest of the family for not acting sooner. This would have been a valid response, and I would have gotten agreement and sympathy from my friends and acquaintances. I almost went down this path until I decided to play my mindful game of thriving even under these conditions. I chose to experience my love for my dad instead of my fear for his condition.

You may be thinking that it happened for me but won't happen for you. If you have that belief, you will prove it true. But a better belief you can choose is "If it worked for her, it is possible that it will work for me too." That is a belief with more possibility, and you are more likely to experiment with the concepts in this book and get results that move you toward what you prefer.

When you have made thriving your habit and you choose to focus on what you want instead of proving that you can't have what you want and who is at fault, the fun and excitement of life gets bigger and fuller, and the fun continues to expand. Everything that happens is an opportunity to choose.

To choose to thrive.

Are you ready?

Then let's get into the big game.

CHAPTER 9

The Big Game

What if the need to fight against an enemy became obsolete? That's hard to imagine.

It was for me, too—before having the model to highlight the options and choices that were always there but I was not able to see. It is hard to see or even believe better choices can exist when we are constantly being told of the dangers out there. You can't turn on the television, drive down the street, or get on Facebook without seeing a message that is warning you about all the enemies around the corner that need to be avoided or destroyed. Every conspiracy, disease, or social mishap is given the same degree of contempt and level of threat. It is hard to imagine that we can survive life without the need to have those threats be our primary focus.

Recently, I felt myself going into survival mode after watching a video that was describing how a few powerful people were planning to grab global control of all the world's resources and ultimately all the people. The video claimed documented proof that things were moving in a dire direction, and I felt a level of hopelessness. How do you prevent people with all that power from doing whatever it is that they want?

It is sometimes overwhelming to think about how to win a game that you don't even want to be in. To try to fight against the powers that be would only keep me in a game of survival, pushing against what I don't want and being distracted from the vision of a future that I do want.

We humans have made up the rules to the game of our economy, business, and government. It is by our agreement with how the game is played that it keeps being played in the same way no matter the consequence to us and the rest of the earth. The agreement in the belief that there is not enough to go around so you need to grab all you can before someone else does keeps us in a state of fear, and our filters stay set to look for all the proof that this is true and discard any evidence to the contrary.

We believe this even though more people in the world (and especially in the Western world) are existing at a higher standard of living according to a recent World Bank study (Feeney, 2012)—a decline from 40 to about 14 percent of the world's population suffering from abject want from 1980 to 2010. And poverty rates are declining in every national income bracket. Even in low-income countries, the percentage of people living in extreme poverty ($1.25 a day in 2005 dollars) has gone down from 63 in 1981 to 44 in 2010. That does not negate the fact that there is still poverty and a wide gap between the haves and have-nots. However, it does indicate that the trend is moving in a better direction than most of us know or is highlighted.

We are still operating, as a species, from a perspective of lack— that there is not enough to go around. This has been our big drama, and as individuals, we are playing it out in our day-to-day lives, and it has us feel we are in constant us-versus-them survival mode.

What if we don't have to keep playing the us-versus-them survival game? What if we changed our big game to one of thriving, of knowing and realizing the abundance that the earth has provided, and focusing on how we all can benefit instead of getting all we can before it's all gone?

Notice what thoughts and beliefs pop into your head to give you proof that even if that is a world you prefer, it isn't possible. Even though it feels more right to be focused on going toward something that we want and doing things that we prefer, we still have beliefs that we have bought into without question, without gathering from our own experiences. It is these thoughts and unexamined beliefs that have us give up looking for solutions and behaving any differently.

We have been in this mode of survival for a very long time; it almost seems impossible to imagine it could be any other way.

But that is the key. To get to a place where we can imagine it is possible to thrive and not just survive.

Because I have experienced the transformation of seeing people I once thought of as evil enemies into fellow human beings I can respect, other people on their own journeys, even if I don't agree or prefer the game they are playing, I no longer have a need to fight against them as enemies. I have reached a point where I no longer have the need or desire to see anyone or anything as an enemy. I experience this as true.

I also know that if I can experience the freedom of staying focused on thriving and not having to prove to others who don't agree, or condemn those who believe and act differently, I know it is possible for others to reach that point too.

But how can I, just one person, make a difference in the big game of society?

When I see that I can change the game in my life, play a game of mindful thriving, and can appreciate and love others unconditionally, I can imagine that it could work with the people around me. And if I can imagine it working for the people around me, I can begin to imagine it working for the world and know that it is possible.

When we look to see how the world can work and believe that it is possible and worth our time and effort, we begin to see solutions, opportunities, and actions that we can take to move us in that direction. We can truly imagine the real possibility of a world where the majority of people's focus is on how to make the world a better place for all instead of how to protect their wealth and power or make a better weapon so that they can control what others do or believe.

If I had seen that disturbing video before I had the model and known that I get to decide which game I want to be in, it would have fed the underlying helplessness and hopelessness that had seemed to always be there. Now I use those uncomfortable feelings as a signal of a coming new insight. It reminds me to imagine how I would prefer the world to be and look for evidence that there are those out there who know more about economy, technology, and other disciplines that are taking actions toward a better future they prefer and not just trying to fight against the way things are.

By thriving in your day-to-day life, experiencing that there is a different way, you are contributing to all of humanity.

There are many examples of those who follow their callings and find avenues to do what they love because they don't get distracted by the beliefs and agreement of how life is—scientists, inventors, artists, musicians, and entrepreneurs who stepped out of the societal beliefs and were accused of not being normal.

Many were called crazy and ridiculed, or they were encouraged to stop by those who were their loved ones and wanted to support them in winning at a game they were not interested in playing. They instead made their game of following what came naturally to them, learning and growing in their unique talents and perspectives, and it is those people who have changed the world.

There are many examples of people who have given up on doing what they really love because they bought into the belief that life was about struggle and doing what someone else wanted them to do in order to make a living, in order to survive. They needed to fit in, not rock the boat, and be approved of by those around them—those who have caught on to the fear that there is not enough to go around and so need to find a way to make a living instead of pursuing what brings them their most excitement. And it is these people who are miserable, stressed out, and fearful, who are telling their children and those around them the same story of how life supposedly is.

As Buckminster Fuller stated, we need to stop being afraid of those who are afraid.

The only way for the collective conscious to have the ability to decide to play a mindful game of thriving is when an individual sees it is possible and plays.

We can only change our perspectives, live our lives thriving, and influence others with our example. To believe that we need to make them do anything because we believe we are right will put us right back into survival mode and drama. We need to choose and let others choose and appreciate that people deal with their own unconscious beliefs like we do.

To mindfully play a game of thriving—not comparing or trying to show up others so that we don't lose out, but finding our joy and lining up our goals and actions—is what will change the world and create opportunity for a better future. We make a difference when we choose what we believe because of what we prefer. When we change our focus, we change our world, and we also influence the world of those around us. And this new perspective will grow like a virus. Stop being afraid or condemning others who are afraid and condemning.

We do not give ourselves credit for how amazing we are. Instead of creating, our energy is put into proving our limitations. We study what is wrong and think it will tell us what works. We study brain damage and think it will tell us about a healthy brain. We study sickness and believe that it is teaching us about a healthy person. This has not created more health but more and newer diseases. We are scaring ourselves, and there are more hospitals than ever.

We are being told what is normal, but is there really ever a normal if each of us has a unique perspective, body, and set of beliefs? And why is normal a desirable state? Most of us have to go against what feels natural for us in order to feel normal, so what is the reward? That we are accepted by people who conditionally accept us if we match what they want? Is that really acceptance? We are in the same trap.

Fulfillment and happiness come from creating, finding what we uniquely have to bring and explore and dream and grow.

How many humans had it in them to create beneficial things and didn't pursue them because they had to make a living and so got jobs in sales or other fields that were not their true callings?

The change will not come from toppling the current setup. It won't come from political action, and it won't come from trying to stamp out those who don't agree or who are the "bad leaders." As Brother David Steindl-Rast, a Benedictine monk, talks about in his TED talk about gratefulness, we need a revolution—not the revolution where you turn the pyramid upside down and the oppressed end up becoming the oppressors, but a revolution of networking. Where we are reaching out to those around us with appreciation and seeing the opportunities to enjoy and grow and contribute in a world of enough instead of one of scarcity (Steindl-Rast, 2013).

This creates joyful people, and the more joyful people there are, the more the world becomes a joyful world.

A world that thrives.

Works Cited

Ariely, D. (2012, October). *What makes us feel good about our work?* Retrieved 2013, from TED.Com: http://www.ted.com/talks/ dan_ariely_what_makes_us_feel_good_about_our_work

Barsade, S., & Gibson, O. E. (1998). Group Emotion: A View from Top and Bottom. In D. Gruenfeld, M. Neale, & E. Mannix, *Research on Managing in Groups and Teams* (pp. 81-102). Greenwich, CT: JAI Press.

Beersma, B., Hollenbeck, J. R., Humphrey, S. E., Moon, H., Conlon, D. E., & Iigen, D. R. (2003). Cooperation, Competition, And Team Performance Toward A Contingency Approach. *Academy of Management Journal, 46*(5), 572-590.

Blue, L. (2012, November 14). *Strongest Study Yet Shows Meditation Can Lower Risk of Heart Attack and Stroke.* Retrieved October 30, 2014, from Time.com: http://healthland.time.com/2012/11/14/ mind-over-matter-strongest-study-yet-shows-meditation-can-lower-risk-of-heart-attack-and-stroke/

Deutsch, M. (1949). An Experimental Study of the Effects of Co-operation Upon Group Process. *Human RElations*, 199-232.

Feeney, L. (2012, March 7). *Extreme Poverty Down Globally, Up in U.S.* Retrieved 2013, from Moyers and Company: http://billmoyers. com/2012/03/07/extreme-poverty-down-globally-up-in-u-s/

Fehr, E., & Schmidt, K. M. (1999). Theory of Fairness, Competition and Cooperation. *The Quarterly Journal of Economics*, 817-868.

Fredrickson, B. L. (2004). The Broaden-and-Build Theory of Positive Emotions. *The Royal Society*, 1367-1377.

Freeman, W. J. (1995). *Societies of the Brain*. Hillsdale, NJ: Lawrence Erlbaum Associates.

Friedman, H., & Riggio, R. (1981). Effect of Individual Differences in Nonverbal Expressiveness on Transmission of Emotions. *Journal of Nonverbal Behavior, 6*, 32-58.

Huayao, Z., & Xiaokun, S. (2011). Cooperation and Innovation of Japanese Enterprises: The Investigation from Firm-Level and Project-Level. *Science Research Management* .

Jhensen, E. (1995). *The Learning Brain*. San Diego: Turning Point Publishing.

Kagan, S., & Knight, G. P. (1979, December). Cooperation-Competition and Self-Esteem: A Case of Cultural Relativisim. *Journal of Cross-Cultural Psychology, 10*(4), 457-467.

Kohn, A. (1986). *No Contest: The Case Against Competition*. New York: Houghton Mufflin Company.

McGonigal, J. (2011). *Reality Is Broken: Why Games Make Us Better and How They Can Change the World* . New York: Penquin Books.

Merriam-Webster. (n.d.). *http://www.learnersdictionary.com/ definition/thrive*. Retrieved June 2014, from http://www. learnersdictionary.com: http://www.learnersdictionary.com

Open University. (2010, September 21). *Appearance and reality: in conversation with Derren Brown - OU Boundaries philosophy series* . Retrieved 2013, from YouTube: https://www.youtube. com/watch?v=U1cMmz7m3AA

Steindl-Rast, D. (2013, June). *Want to be Happy? Be Grateful*. Retrieved 2013, from TED.com: http://www.ted.com/talks/ david_steindl_rast_want_to_be_happy_be_grateful

Thompson, V. (2013, April 24). *Energy Efficient Brain Simulator Outperforms Supercomputers*. Retrieved 2013, from National Science Foundation: http://www.nsf.gov/discoveries/ disc_summ.jsp?cntn_id=127617&org=NSF

Wilson, T. D. (2009). *Strangers to Ourselves*. Boston: Harvard University Press.

Printed in the United States
By Bookmasters